MW01200910

enVision® Integrated

MATHEMATICS I

Student Companion

SAVVAS
LEARNING COMPANY

Savvas Learning Company LLC, 15 East Midland Avenue, Paramus, NJ 07652

SAVVAS
LEARNING COMPANY

ISBN-13: 978-1-4183-1
ISBN-10: 1-4183-1
5

ontents

enVision Integrated MATHEMATICS I

About the Authors

Authors

Dan Kennedy, Ph.D

- Classroom teacher and the Lupton Distinguished Professor of Mathematics at the Baylor School in Chattanooga, TN
- Co-author of textbooks *Precalculus: Graphical, Numerical, Algebraic* and *Calculus: Graphical, Numerical, Algebraic, AP Edition*
- Past chair of the College Board's AP Calculus Development Committee.
- Previous Tandy Technology Scholar and Presidential Award winner

Eric Milou, Ed.D

- Professor of Mathematics, Rowan University, Glassboro, NJ
- Member of the author team for Savvas' **enVision**math**2.0** 6-8
- Member of National Council of Teachers of Mathematics (NCTM) feedback/advisory team for the Common Core State Standards
- Author of *Teaching Mathematics to Middle School Students*

Christine D. Thomas, Ph.D

- Professor of Mathematics Education at Georgia State University, Atlanta, GA
- Past-President of the Association of Mathematics Teacher Educators (AMTE)
- Past NCTM Board of Directors Member
- Past member of the editorial panel of the NCTM journal *Mathematics Teacher*
- Past co-chair of the steering committee of t North American chapter of the Internation Group of the Psychology of Mathematics Education

Rose Mary Zbiek, Ph.D

- Professor of Mathematics Education, Pennsylvania State University, College Park, PA
- Series editor for the NCTM *Essential Understanding* project

Contributing Author

Al Cuoco, Ph.D

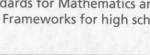

- Lead author of CME Project, a National Science Foundation (NSF)-funded high school curriculum
- Team member to revise the Conference Board of the Mathematical Sciences (CBMS) recommendations for teach preparation and professional development
- Co-author of several books published by the Mathematical Association of America and t American Mathematical Society
- Consultant to the writers of the Common Core State Standards for Mathematics and t PARCC Content Frameworks for high school mathematics

1-1 Solving Linear Equations

SavvasRealize.com

MODEL & DISCUSS

Joshua is going kayaking with a group during one of his vacation days. In his vacation planning, he budgeted $50 for a kayak rental.

A. How can Joshua determine the number of hours he can rent a kayak for himself? Describe two different options.

B. Joshua found out that there is a $25 nonrefundable equipment fee in addition to the hourly rates. How does this requirement change the mathematics of the situation?

C. **Look for Relationships** How do the processes you used for parts A and B differ? How are they the same?

HABITS OF MIND

Make Sense and Persevere How did you determine which operations are needed to solve the problem?

Notes

Assess

EXAMPLE 1

Try It! Solve Linear Equations

1. Solve the equation $4 + \frac{3x - 1}{2} = 9$. Explain the reasons why you chose your solution method.

HABITS OF MIND

Communicate Precisely How can you check that the value of the variable makes the equation true?

EXAMPLE 2

Try It! Solve Consecutive Integer Problems

2. The sum of three consecutive odd integers is 57. What are the three integers?

EXAMPLE 3

Try It! Use Linear Equations to Solve Mixture Problems

3. If the lab technician needs 30 liters of a 25% acid solution, how many liters of the 10% and the 30% acid solutions should she mix to get what she needs?

EXAMPLE 4

Try It! Use Linear Equations to Solve Problems

4. The same four friends buy tickets for two shows on consecutive nights. They use a coupon for $5 off each ticket. They pay a total of $416 for 8 tickets. Write and solve an equation to find the original price of the tickets.

EXAMPLE 5

Try It! Solve Work and Time Problems

5. LaTanya leaves her house at 12:30 P.M. and bikes at 12 mi/h to Marta's house. She stays at Marta's house for 90 min. Both girls walk back to LaTanya's house at 2.5 mi/h. They arrive at LaTanya's house at 3:30 P.M. How far is Marta's house from LaTanya's house?

HABITS OF MIND

Look for Relationships What patterns can you identify in the solutions for Examples 3, 4, and 5?

Assess

Do You UNDERSTAND?

1. ESSENTIAL QUESTION How do you create equations and use them to solve problems?

2. **Reason** What is a first step to solving for x in the equation $9x - 7 = 10$? How would you check your solution?

3. **Use Structure** For an equation with fractions, why is it helpful to multiply both sides of the equation by the LCD?

4. **Error Analysis** Venetta knows that 1 mi ≈ 1.6 km. To convert 5 mi/h to km/h, she multiplies 5 mi/h by $\frac{1 \text{ mi}}{1.6 \text{ km}}$. What error does Venetta make?

Do You KNOW HOW?

Solve each equation.

5. $4b + 14 = 22$

6. $-6k - 3 = 39$

7. $15 - 2(3 - 2x) = 46$

8. $\frac{2}{3}y - \frac{2}{5} = 5$

9. **Mathematical Modeling** Terrence walks at a pace of 2 mi/h to the theater and watches a movie for 2 h and 15 min. He rides back home, taking the same route, on the bus that travels at a rate of 40 mi/h. The entire trip takes 3.5 h. How far along this route is Terrence's house from the theater? Explain.

Activity

1-2 Solving Equations With a Variable on Both Sides

SavvasRealize.com

EXPLORE & REASON

Some friends want to see a movie that is showing at two different theaters in town. They plan to share 3 tubs of popcorn during the movie.

	Theater A	Theater B
Ticket Price	\$14.50	\$13.00
Popcorn	\$5.75	\$6.75

A. Construct Arguments Which movie theater should the friends choose? Explain.

B. For what situation would the total cost at each theater be exactly the same? Explain.

C. There are different methods to solving this problem. Which do you think is the best? Why?

HABITS OF MIND

Make Sense and Persevere What assumptions did you make that helped you work through the Explore & Reason?

Notes

Assess

EXAMPLE 1

Try It! Solve Equations With a Variable on Both Sides

1. Solve each equation.

a. $100(z - 0.2) = -10(5z + 0.8)$

b. $\frac{5}{8}(16d + 24) = 6(d - 1) + 1$

EXAMPLE 2

Try It! Understand Equations with Infinitely Many or No Solutions

2. Solve each equation. Is the equation an identity? Explain.

a. $t - 27 = -(27 - t)$

b. $16(4 - 3m) = 96\left(-\frac{m}{2} + 1\right)$

HABITS OF MIND

Construct Arguments One student maintains that the order in which terms are collected on each side of an equation does not matter. Construct an argument to support or refute the student's position.

Notes

Assess

EXAMPLE 3

Try It! Solve Mixture Problems

3. How many pounds of Arabica coffee should you mix with 5 pounds of Robusta coffee to make a coffee blend that costs $12.00 per pound?

HABITS OF MIND

Generalize How can you determine whether an equation has infinitely many or no solutions?

EXAMPLE 4

Try It! Use Equations to Solve Problems

4. Cameron's friend tells him of another service that has a $15 joining fee but charges $0.80 per song. At what number of songs does this new service become a less expensive option to Cameron's current service?

Do You UNDERSTAND?

1. **ESSENTIAL QUESTION** How do you create equations with a variable on both sides and use them to solve problems?

2. **Vocabulary** Why does it make sense to describe an equation that has infinitely many solutions as an *identity*?

3. **Error Analysis** Isabel says that the equation $x - 2 = -(x - 2)$ has no solution because a number can never be equal to its opposite. Explain the error Isabel made.

4. **Look for Relationships** You are solving an equation with a variable on each side. Does the side on which you choose to isolate the variable affect the solution? Why might you choose one side over the other?

Do You KNOW HOW?

Solve each equation.

5. $5(2x + 6) = 8x + 48$

6. $-3(8 + 3h) = 5h + 4$

7. $2(y - 6) = 3(y - 4) - y$

8. $8x - 4 = 2(4x - 4)$

9. For how many games is the total cost of bowling equal for the two bowling establishments?

Family Bowling

Cost (dollars)	Game	4.00
	Shoes	1.00

Knight Owl Bowling

Cost (dollars)	Game	3.75
	Shoes	2.00

Activity

1-3 Literal Equations and Formulas

SavvasRealize.com

MODEL & DISCUSS

Nora drew a nonsquare rectangle. Then she drew the length of each side from end to end to make a line segment to represent the perimeter.

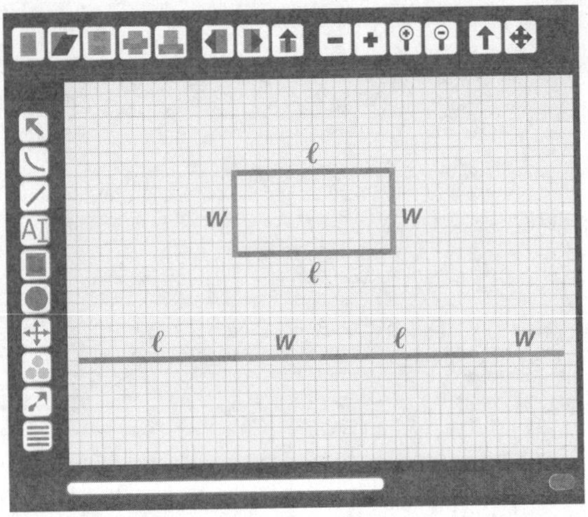

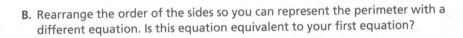

A. Write an equation that represents the perimeter of the model shown.

B. Rearrange the order of the sides so you can represent the perimeter with a different equation. Is this equation equivalent to your first equation?

C. Use Structure How many different ways can you express the relationship in parts A and B? Are any of them more useful than others?

HABITS OF MIND

Construct Arguments What mathematical argument supports your response in part C?

Notes

Assess

EXAMPLE 1

Try It! Rewrite Literal Equations

1. What equation can Janet use to calculate the principal amount?

EXAMPLE 2

Try It! Use Literal Equations to Solve Problems

2. Sarah is going to the store 2.5 miles away. She has only 15 min to get there before they close. At what average speed must she ride to get to the store before they close?

HABITS OF MIND

Use Structure How is solving equations with numbers the same as solving equations with only variables?

Assess

EXAMPLE 3

Try It! Rewrite a Formula

3. Write the formula for the area of a triangle, $A = \frac{1}{2}bh$ in terms of h. Find the height of a triangle when $A = 18$ in.^{2} and $b = 9$ in.

EXAMPLE 4

Try It! Apply Formulas

4. The high temperature on a given winter day is 5°F. What is the temperature in °C?

HABITS OF MIND

Reason How are the variables in the temperature conversion formula related?

Assess

Do You UNDERSTAND?

1. ESSENTIAL QUESTION How is rewriting literal equations useful when solving problems?

2. **Communicate Precisely** How is solving $2x + c = d$ similar to solving $2x + 1 = 9$ for x? How are they different? How can you use $2x + c = d$ to solve $2x + 1 = 9$?

3. **Vocabulary** Explain how literal equations and formulas are related.

4. **Error Analysis** Dyani began solving the equation $g = \frac{x-1}{k}$ for x by using the Addition Property of Equality. Explain Dyani's error. Then describe how to solve for x.

Do You KNOW HOW?

Solve each literal equation for the given variable.

5. $y = x + 12$; x

6. $n = \frac{4}{5}(m + 7)$; m

7. Use your equation from Exercise 6 to find m when $n = 40$.

8. William got scores of q_1, q_2, and q_3 on three quizzes.

   a. Write a formula for the average x of all three quizzes.

   b. William got an 85 and an 88 on the first two quizzes. What formula can William use to determine the score he needs on the third quiz to get an average of 90? What score does he need?

Activity

1-4 Solving Inequalities in One Variable

SavvasRealize.com

MODEL & DISCUSS

Skyler competes in the high jump event at her school. She hopes to tie or break some records at the next meet.

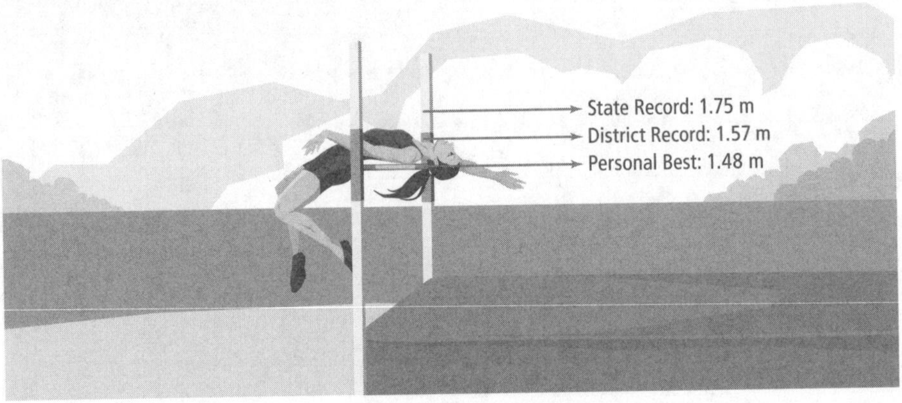

A. Write and solve an equation to find *x*, the number of meters Skyler must add to her personal best to tie the district record.

B. **Look for Relationships** Rewrite your equation as an inequality to represent the situation where Skyler *breaks* the district record. How is the value of *x* in the inequality related to the value of *x* in the equation?

C. How many meters does Skyler need to add to her personal best to break the state record?

HABITS OF MIND

Make Sense and Persevere What strategy did you use to answer the questions? What other strategy might you have used?

Assess

EXAMPLE 1

Try It! Solve Inequalities

1. Solve each inequality and graph the solution.

   a. $-3(2x + 2) < 10$

   b. $2(4 - 2x) > 1$

EXAMPLE 2

Try It! Solve an Inequality With Variables on Both Sides

2. Solve $2x - 5 < 5x - 22$. Then graph the solution.

EXAMPLE 3

Try It! Understand Inequalities With Infinitely Many or No Solutions

3. Solve each inequality.

a. $-2(4x - 2) < -8x + 4$

b. $-6x - 5 < -3(2x + 1)$

EXAMPLE 4

Try It! Use Inequalities to Solve Problems

4. If Florist B increases the cost per rose to $5.20, for what number of roses is it less expensive to order from Florist A? From Florist B?

HABITS OF MIND

Look for Structure How is solving an inequality with variables on one side similar to and different from solving an inequality with variables on both sides?

Do You UNDERSTAND?

1. ESSENTIAL QUESTION How are the solutions of an inequality different from the solution of an equation?

2. **Reason** How is dividing each side of $x > 0$ by a negative value different from dividing each side by a positive value?

3. **Vocabulary** Give an example of two inequalities that are *equivalent inequalities*. Explain your reasoning.

4. **Error Analysis** Rachel multiplied each side of $x \geq 2$ by 3. She wrote the result as $3x \leq 6$. Explain the error Rachel made.

Do You KNOW HOW?

Solve each inequality and graph the solution.

5. $\frac{1}{2}x < 6$

6. $-4x \geq 20$

7. $8 \leq -4(x - 1)$

8. $3x - 2 > 4 - 3x$

9. Lourdes plans to jog at least 1.5 miles. Write and solve an inequality to find x, the number of hours that Lourdes will have to jog.

Video

MATHEMATICAL MODELING IN 3 ACTS

SavvasRealize.com

Collecting Cans

Many schools and community centers organize canned food drives and donate the food collected to area food pantries or homeless shelters.

A teacher may hold a contest for the student who collects the most cans. The teacher will track the number of cans each student brings in. Sometimes students have their own ways of keeping track. You'll see how some students kept track in the Mathematical Modeling in 3 Acts lesson.

ACT 1

1. What is the first question that comes to mind after watching the video?

2. Write down the Main Question you will answer.

3. Make an initial conjecture that answers this Main Question.

4. Explain how you arrived at your conjecture.

5. Write a number that you know is too small.

6. Write a number that you know is too large.

Video

ACT 2

7. Use the math that you have learned in the topic to refine your conjecture.

ACT 3

8. Is your refined conjecture between the highs and lows you set up earlier?

9. Did your refined conjecture match the actual answer exactly? If not, what might explain the difference?

Activity

1-5 Compound Inequalities

SavvasRealize.com

EXPLORE & REASON

Hana has some blue paint. She wants to lighten the shade, so she mixes in 1 cup of white paint. The color is still too dark, so Hana keeps mixing in 1 cup of white paint at a time. After adding 4 cups, she decides the color is too light.

A. Explain in words how much paint Hana should have added initially to get the shade she wants.

B. **Model With Mathematics** Represent your answer to part A with one or more inequalities.

C. Hana decides that she likes the shades of blue that appear in between adding 1 cup and 4 cups of white paint. How can you represent the number of cups of white paint that yield the shades Hana prefers?

HABITS OF MIND

Mathematical Modeling If the solution to an inequality includes all the values that are in between two values, how can you show that on a number line?

EXAMPLE 1

Try It! Understand Compound Inequalities

1. Write a compound inequality for the graph.

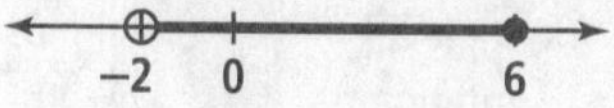

EXAMPLE 2

Try It! Solve a Compound Inequality Involving *Or*

2. Solve the compound inequality $-3x + 2 > -7$ or $2(x - 2) \geq 6$. Graph the solution.

HABITS OF MIND

Make Sense of Problems How does representing a compound inequality solution on a graph help show the solution accurately?

Notes

Assess

EXAMPLE 3

Try It! Solve a Compound Inequality Involving *And*

3. Solve the compound inequality $-2(x + 1) < 4$ and $4x + 1 \leq -3$. Graph the solution.

EXAMPLE 4

Try It! Solve Problems Involving Compound Inequalities

4. Suppose River has new treats that are 10 calories each. How many of the new treats can she have and remain in her calorie range?

HABITS OF MIND

Communicate Precisely Describe the solution of an inequality involving *or* and an inequality involving *and*.

Do You UNDERSTAND?

1. ESSENTIAL QUESTION What are compound inequalities and how are their solutions represented?

2. **Look for Relationships** When $a < b$, how is the graph of $x > a$ and $x < b$ similar to the graph of $x > a$? How is it different?

3. **Vocabulary** A *compound* is defined as a *mixture*. Make a conjecture as to why the term *compound inequality* includes the word *compound*.

4. **Error Analysis** Kona graphed the compound inequality $x > 2$ or $x > 3$ by graphing $x > 3$. Explain Kona's error.

Do You KNOW HOW?

Write a compound inequality for each graph.

5.
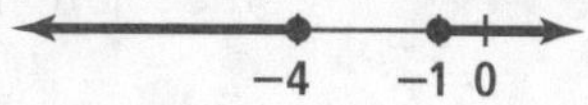

6.
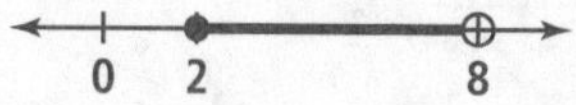

Solve each compound inequality and graph the solution.

7. $4x - 1 > 3$ and $-2(3x - 4) \geq -16$

8. $2(4x + 3) \geq -10$ or $-5x - 15 > 5$

9. Nadeem plans to ride her bike between 12 mi and at most 15 mi. Write and solve an inequality to model how many hours Nadeem will be riding.

Activity

1-6 Absolute Value Equations and Inequalities

SavvasRealize.com

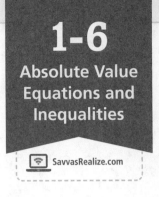

MODEL & DISCUSS

Amelia is participating in a 60-mile spin-a-thon. Her spin bike keeps track of the simulated number of miles she travels. She plans to take a 15-minute break within 5 miles of riding 30 miles.

Amelia spins at a constant 22 mph.

Spin-a-thon Schedule	
Event	**Time**
Start spinning	10:00 A.M.
Stop for break	■
Resume spinning	■

A. Write a compound inequality that models the number of miles Amelia spins before taking a break.

B. How is the number of miles Amelia spins before she takes a break related to the amount of time before she takes a break?

C. Make Sense and Persevere About how many hours will Amelia spin before she takes a break? Discuss how you could use your mathematical model to complete the spin-a-thon schedule.

HABITS OF MIND

Reason How is the time Amelia is spinning related to the distance she spins?

Notes

Assess

EXAMPLE 1

Try It! Understand Absolute Value Equations

1. Solve.

a. $6 = |x| - 2$ b. $2|x + 5| = 4$ c. $|3x - 6| = 12$

EXAMPLE 2

Try It! Apply an Absolute Value Equation

2. What will be the minimum and maximum time that Kennedy will travel if she resets her cruising speed to 20 mi/h?

HABITS OF MIND

Generalize How is solving an absolute value equation similar to solving a regular equation? How is it different?

EXAMPLE 3

Try It! Understand Absolute Value Inequalities

3. Solve and graph the solutions of each inequality.

a. $|x| > 15$

b. $|x| \leq 7$

EXAMPLE 4

Try It! Write an Absolute Value Inequality

4. If the debate team increased their limit to \$200 plus or minus \$20, would they be able to afford Hotel D at \$55 per night? Explain.

HABITS OF MIND

Look for Relationships What do you notice about absolute value inequalities that is similar to compound inequalities?

Do You UNDERSTAND?

1. ESSENTIAL QUESTION Why does the solution for an absolute value equation or inequality typically result in a pair of equations or inequalities?

2. **Reason** How is solving an absolute value equation similar to solving an equation that does not involve absolute value? How is it different?

3. **Vocabulary** Describe how you would explain to another student why the *absolute value* of a number cannot be negative.

4. **Error Analysis** Yumiko solved $|x| > 5$ by solving $x > -5$ and $x < 5$. Explain the error Yumiko made.

Do You KNOW HOW?

Solve each absolute value equation.

5. $5 = |x| + 3$

6. $|2x - 8| = 16$

Solve each absolute value inequality. Graph the solution.

7. $|3x - 6| \geq 9$

8. $|4x - 12| \leq 20$

9. On a road trip, Andrew plans to use his cruise control for 125 mi, plus or minus 20 mi. Write and solve an equation to find the minimum and maximum number of hours for Andrew's road trip.

Activity

2-1 Slope–Intercept Form

SavvasRealize.com

MODEL & DISCUSS

Alani wants to buy a $360 bicycle. She is considering two payment options. The image shows Option A, which consists of making an initial down payment then smaller, equal-sized weekly payments. Option B consists of making 6 equal payments over 6 weeks.

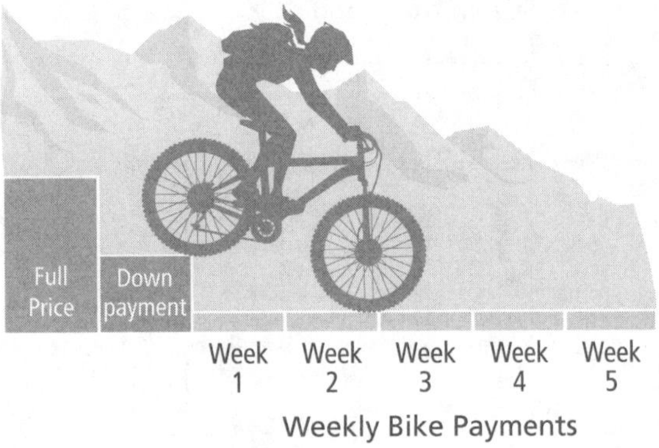

A. What factors should Alani take into consideration before deciding between Option A and Option B?

B. Communicate Precisely Suppose Alani could modify Option A and still pay off the bike in 5 weeks. Describe the relationship between the down payment and the weekly payments.

HABITS OF MIND

Look for Relationships What do you notice about the relationship among the amount of the payment, the number of payments, and the time it takes to pay off the loan?

EXAMPLE 1

Try It! Graph a Linear Equation

1. Sketch the graph of $y = -\frac{3}{4}x - 5$.

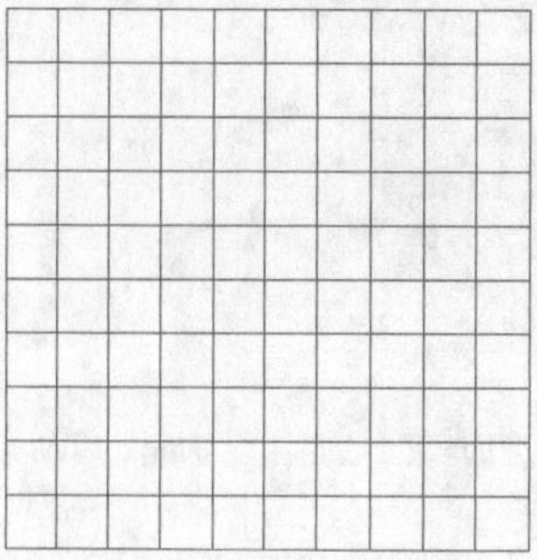

HABITS OF MIND

Reason What do the numbers represent in a linear equation in slope-intercept form?

EXAMPLE 2

Try It! Write an Equation from a Graph

2. Write the equation of the line in slope-intercept form.

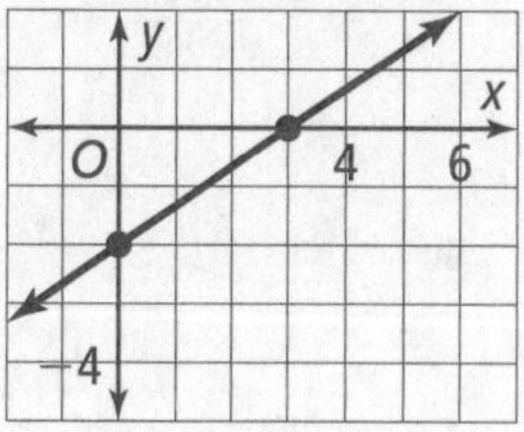

Assess

EXAMPLE 3

Try It! Understand Slope-Intercept Form

3. Write the equation in slope-intercept form of the line that passes through the points (5, 4) and (−1, 6).

EXAMPLE 4

Try It! Interpret Slope and *y*-Intercept

4. Use information from Example 4 to write the equation in slope-intercept form. Find the *x*-intercept of the graph of the equation. What does the *x*-intercept mean in terms of the situation?

HABITS OF MIND

Construct Arguments How does the slope of a line given in slope-intercept form with a fractional coefficient of *x* compare to the slope of a line with a whole number coefficient of *x*?

Do You UNDERSTAND?

1. ESSENTIAL QUESTION What information does the slope-intercept form of a linear equation reveal about a line?

2. **Communicate Precisely** How are the graphs of $y = 2x + 1$ and $y = -2x + 1$ similar? How are they different?

3. **Error Analysis** To graph $y = \frac{2}{3}x + 4$, Emaan plots one point at (0, 4) and a second point 2 units right and 3 units up at (2, 7). He then draws a line through (0, 4) and (2, 7). What error did Emaan make?

4. **Make Sense and Persevere** When writing the equation of a line in slope-intercept form, how can you determine the value of m in $y = mx + b$ if you know the coordinates of two points on the line?

Do You KNOW HOW?

Sketch the graph of each equation.

5. $y = 2x - 5$

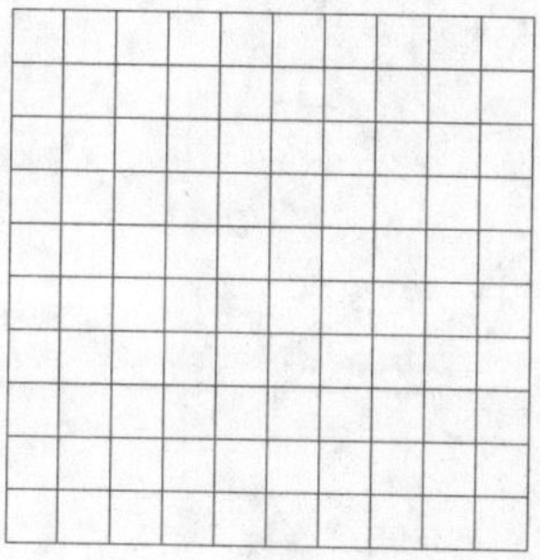

6. $y = -\frac{3}{4}x + 2$

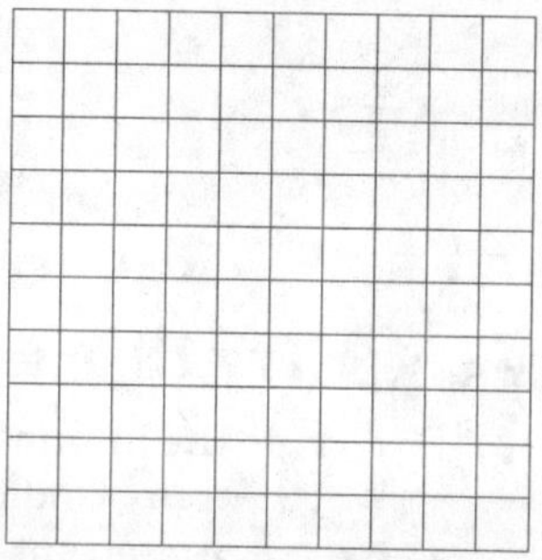

Identify the slope and y-intercept of the line for each equation.

7. $y = -5x - \frac{3}{4}$

8. $y = \frac{1}{4}x + 5$

Write the equation of each line in slope-intercept form.

9.

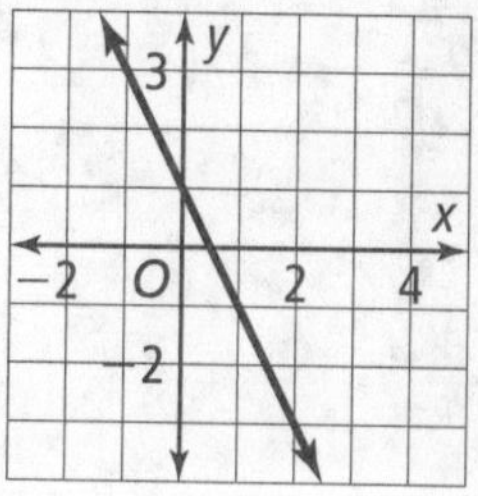

10.

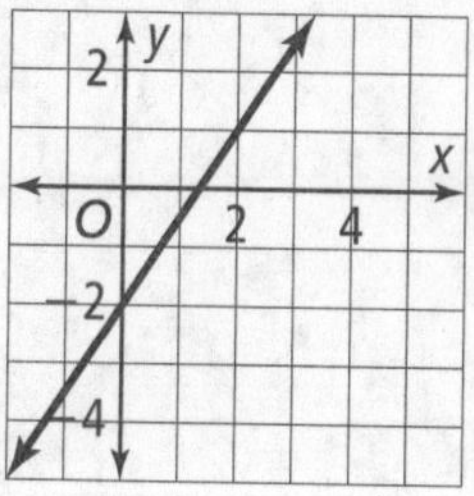

11. A line that passes through (3, 1) and (0, −3)

12. A line that passes through (−1, −5) and (2, 4)

Activity

2-2 Point–Slope Form

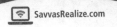

SavvasRealize.com

CRITIQUE & EXPLAIN

Paul and Seth know that one point on a line is (4, 2) and the slope of the line is –5. Each student derived an equation relating *x* and *y*.

Paul

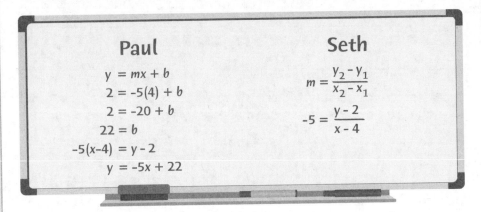

$$y = mx + b$$
$$2 = -5(4) + b$$
$$2 = -20 + b$$
$$22 = b$$
$$-5(x-4) = y - 2$$
$$y = -5x + 22$$

Seth

$$m = \frac{y_2 - y_1}{x_2 - x_1}$$
$$-5 = \frac{y - 2}{x - 4}$$

A. Do the two equations represent the same line? Construct a mathematical argument to support your answer.

B. **Make Sense and Persevere** Generate a table of values for each equation. How can you reconcile the tables with the equations?

HABITS OF MIND

Model With Mathematics How could you represent the equations to show they are equivalent? Explain.

Assess

EXAMPLE 1

Try It! Understand Point–Slope Form of a Linear Equation

1. Describe the steps needed to find the y-intercept of the graph using point-slope form.

EXAMPLE 2

Try It! Write an Equation in Point–Slope Form

2. Write an equation of the line that passes through $(2, -1)$ and $(-3, 3)$.

HABITS OF MIND

Generalize Explain why the equation of a vertical line cannot be written in point–slope form.

EXAMPLE 3 Try It! Sketch the Graph of a Linear Equation in Point-Slope Form

3. Sketch the graph of $y + 2 = \frac{1}{2}(x - 3)$.

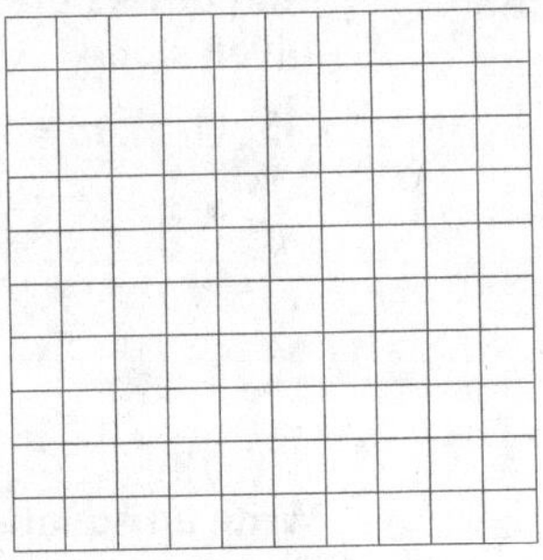

EXAMPLE 4 Try It! Apply Linear Equations

4. Rewrite the point-slope form equation from Example 4 in slope-intercept form. What does the y-intercept represent in terms of the situation?

HABITS OF MIND

Make Sense and Persevere When is it appropriate to write the equation of a line in point-slope form rather than in slope-intercept form?

Do You UNDERSTAND?

1. ESSENTIAL QUESTION What information does the point-slope form of a linear equation reveal about a line?

2. **Use Structure** If you know a point on a line and the slope of the line, how can you find another point on the line?

3. **Error Analysis** Denzel identified (3, 2) as a point on the line $y - 2 = \frac{2}{3}(x + 3)$. What is the error that Denzel made?

4. **Generalize** You know the slope and one point on a line that is not the *y*-intercept. Why might you write the equation in point-slope form instead of slope-intercept form?

Do You KNOW HOW?

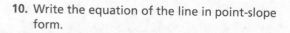

Write the equation of the line in point-slope form that passes through the given point with the given slope.

5. (1, 5); $m = -3$

6. (−4, 3); $m = 2$

Write an equation of the line in point-slope form that passes through the given points.

7. (4, 2) and (1, 6)

8. (−2, 8) and (7, −4)

9. Write the equation $y - 6 = -5(x + 1)$ in slope-intercept form.

10. Write the equation of the line in point-slope form.

a.

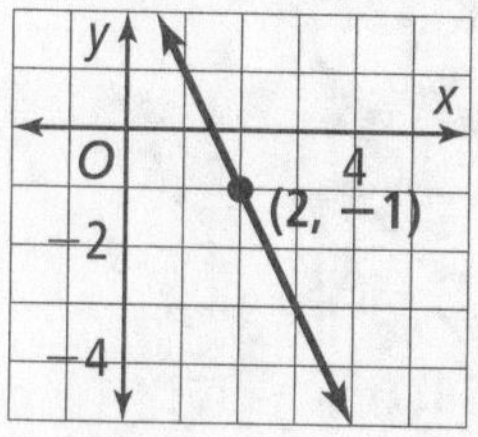

b.

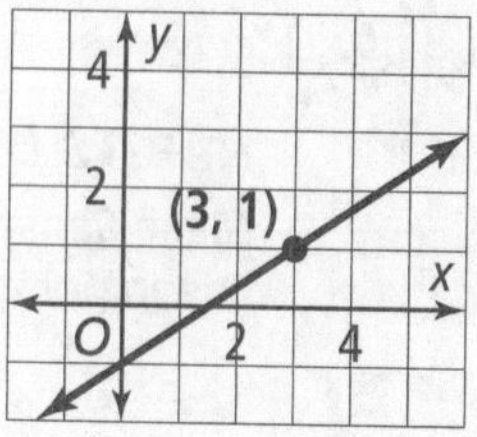

EXPLORE & REASON

Jae makes a playlist of 24 songs for a party. Since he prefers country and rock music, he builds the playlist from those two types of songs.

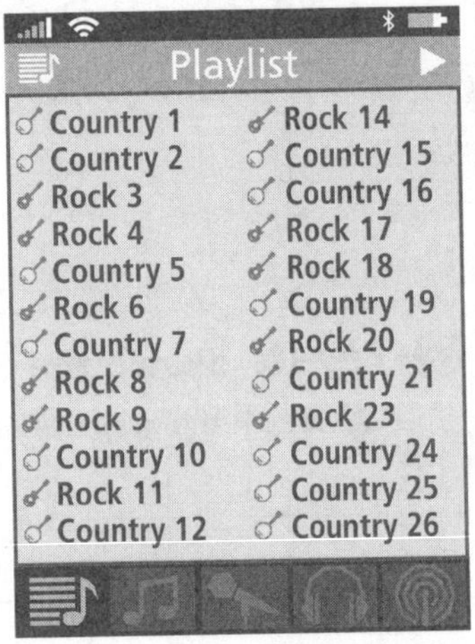

A. Determine two different combinations of country and rock songs that Jae could use for his playlist.

B. Plot those combinations on graph paper. Extend a line through the points.

C. Model With Mathematics Can you use the line to find other meaningful points? Explain.

HABITS OF MIND

Use Appropriate Tools Why is it helpful to use a graph rather than a table to answer the question? Are there any disadvantages to using a graph?

Notes

Assess

EXAMPLE 1

Try It! Understand Standard Form of a Linear Equation

1. Is it easier to find the x-intercept of the graph of the equations in Part B using slope-intercept or standard form? Explain.

EXAMPLE 2

Try It! Sketch the Graph of a Linear Equation in Standard Form

2. Sketch the graph of $4x + 5y = 10$.

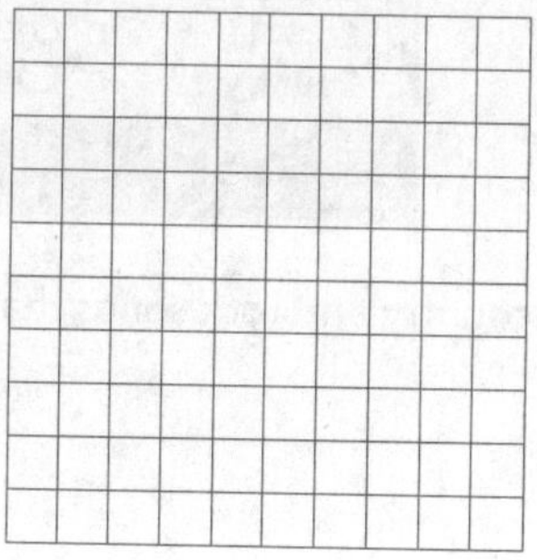

EXAMPLE 3

Try It! Relate Standard Form to Horizontal and Vertical Lines

3. Sketch the graph of each equation.

a. $3y = -18$

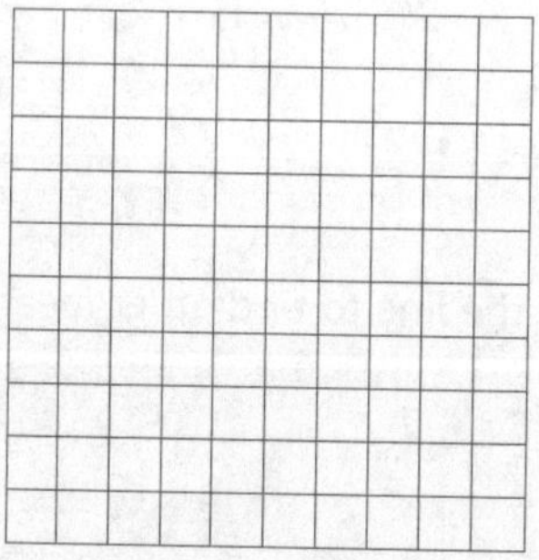

b. $4x = 12$

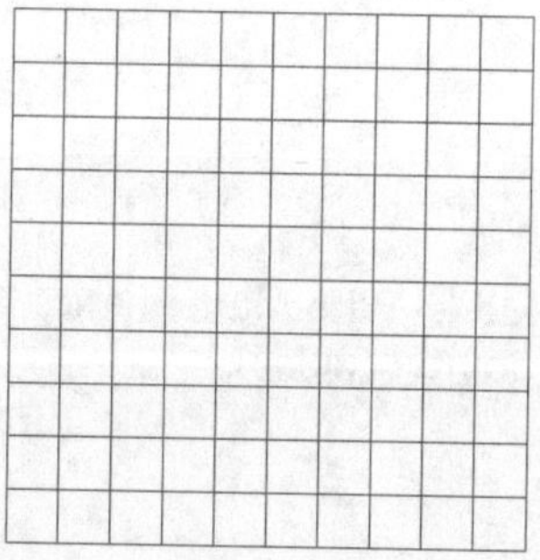

HABITS OF MIND

Generalize Given a linear equation in standard form, can you always find the x- and y-intercepts? Explain.

EXAMPLE 4

Try It! Use the Standard Form of a Linear Equation

4. How does the equation change if Tamira has $60 to spend on a mixture of almonds and cashews? How many pounds of nuts can she buy if she buys only cashews? Only almonds? A mixture of both?

HABITS OF MIND

Model With Mathematics How can you tell when every point on the graph is a solution to the problem?

Do You UNDERSTAND?

1. ESSENTIAL QUESTION What information does the standard form of a linear equation reveal about a line?

2. **Communicate Precisely** How is the standard form of a linear equation similar to and different from the slope-intercept form?

3. **Error Analysis** Malcolm says that $y = -1.5x + 4$ in standard form is $1.5x + y = 4$. What is the error that Malcolm made?

4. **Use Structure** Describe a situation in which the standard form of a linear equation is a more useful than the slope-intercept form.

Do You KNOW HOW?

Use the *x*- and *y*-intercepts to sketch a graph of each equation.

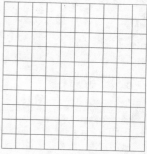

5. $x + 4y = 8$

6. $3x - 4y = 24$

7. $5x = 20$

8. $-3y = 9$

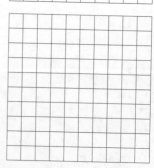

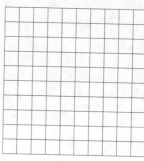

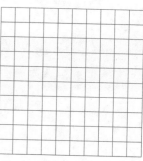

9. Deondra has $12 to spend on a mixture of green and red grapes. What equation can she use to graph a line showing the different amounts of green and red grapes she can buy for $12?

Video

MATHEMATICAL MODELING IN 3 ACTS

SavvasRealize.com

How Tall Is Tall?

The world's tallest person in recorded history was Robert Wadlow. He was 8 feet 11.1 inches tall! Only 5% of the world population is 6 feet 3 inches or taller. What percent of the population would you guess is 7 feet or taller?

We usually use standard units, such as feet and inches or centimeters, to measure length or height. Did you ever wonder why? In the Mathematical Modeling in 3 Acts lesson you'll consider some interesting alternatives.

ACT 1 Identify the Problem

1. What is the first question that comes to mind after watching the video?

2. Write down the main question you will answer about what you saw in the video.

3. Make an initial conjecture that answers this main question.

4. Explain how you arrived at your conjecture.

5. Write a number that you know is too small.

6. Write a number that you know is too large.

7. What information will be useful to know to answer the main question? How can you get it? How will you use that information?

Video

ACT 2 Develop a Model

8. Use the math that you have learned in this Topic to refine your conjecture.

ACT 3 Interpret the Results

9. Is your refined conjecture between the highs and lows you set up earlier?

10. Did your refined conjecture match the actual answer exactly? If not, what might explain the difference?

Activity

2-4 Parallel and Perpendicular Lines

SavvasRealize.com

EXPLORE & REASON

Graph these three equations using a graphing calculator.

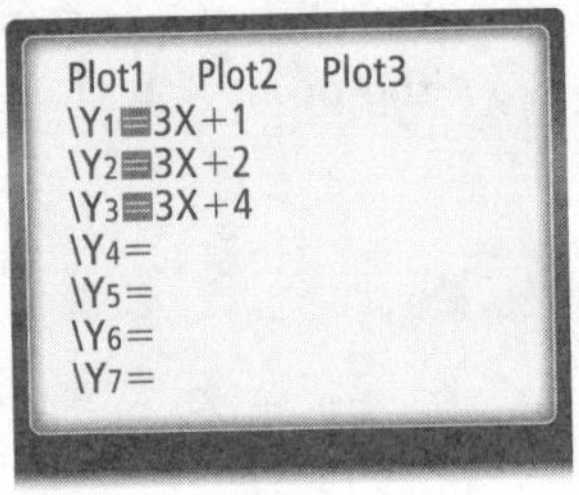

A. Look for Relationships Choose any two of the lines you graphed. How are they related to each other?

B. Does your answer to Part A hold for any two lines? Explain.

C. Write another set of three or more equations that have the same relationships as the first three equations.

HABITS OF MIND

Look for Relationships What concepts have you learned previously that were useful in analyzing this problem?

Notes

Assess

EXAMPLE 1

Try It! Write an Equation of a Parallel Line Parallel to a Given Line

1. Write the equation of the line in slope-intercept form that passes through the point (−3, 5) and is parallel to $y = -\frac{2}{3}x$.

EXAMPLE 2

Try It! Understand the Slopes of Perpendicular Lines

2. Why does it make sense that the slopes of perpendicular lines have opposite signs?

EXAMPLE 3

Try It! Write an Equation of a Line Perpendicular to a Given Line

3. Write the equation of the line that passes through the point (4, 5) and is perpendicular to the graph of $y = 2x - 3$.

HABITS OF MIND

Communicate Precisely Why do you have to use the term "nonvertical" when working with parallel and perpendicular lines?

Notes

Assess

EXAMPLE 4

Try It! Classify Lines

4. Are the graphs of the equations *parallel, perpendicular,* or *neither*?

   a. $y = 2x + 6$ and $y = \frac{1}{2}x + 3$

   b. $y = -5x$ and $25x + 5y = 1$

EXAMPLE 5

Try It! Solve a Real-World Problem

5. The equation $y = 2x + 7$ represents the North Path on a map.

   a. Find the equation for a path that passes through the point (6, 3) and is parallel to the North Path.

   b. Find the equation for a path that passes through the same point but is perpendicular to North Path.

HABITS OF MIND

Use Structure Explain the advantages of using the slope–intercept form of an equation when determining if two lines are perpendicular or parallel to each other.

Assess

Do You UNDERSTAND?

1. **ESSENTIAL QUESTION** How can the equations of lines help you identify whether the lines are *parallel*, *perpendicular*, or *neither*?

2. **Error Analysis** Dwayne stated that the slope of the line perpendicular to $y = -2x$ is 2. Describe Dwayne's error.

3. **Vocabulary** Describe the difference between the slopes of two parallel lines and the slopes of two perpendicular lines.

4. **Use Structure** Is there one line that passes through the point (3, 5) that is parallel to the lines represented by $y = 2x - 4$ and $y = x - 4$? Explain.

Do You KNOW HOW?

The equation $y = -\frac{3}{4}x + 1$ represents a given a line.

5. Write the equation for the line that passes through (−4, 9) and is parallel to the given line.

6. Write the equation for the line that passes through (6, 6) and is perpendicular to the given line.

Are the graphs of the equations parallel, perpendicular, or neither?

7. $x - 3y = 6$ and $x - 3y = 9$

8. $y = 4x + 1$ and $y = -4x - 2$

9. What equation represents the road that that passes through the point shown and is perpendicular to the road represented by the red line?

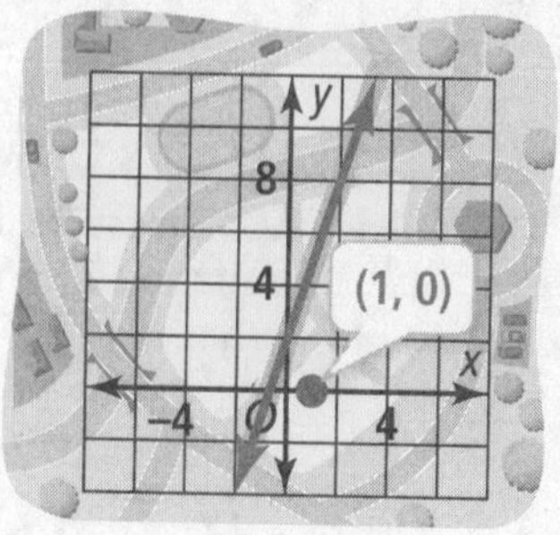

Activity

3-1 Relations and Functions

SavvasRealize.com

EXPLORE & REASON

The desks in a study hall are arranged in rows like the horizontal ones in the picture.

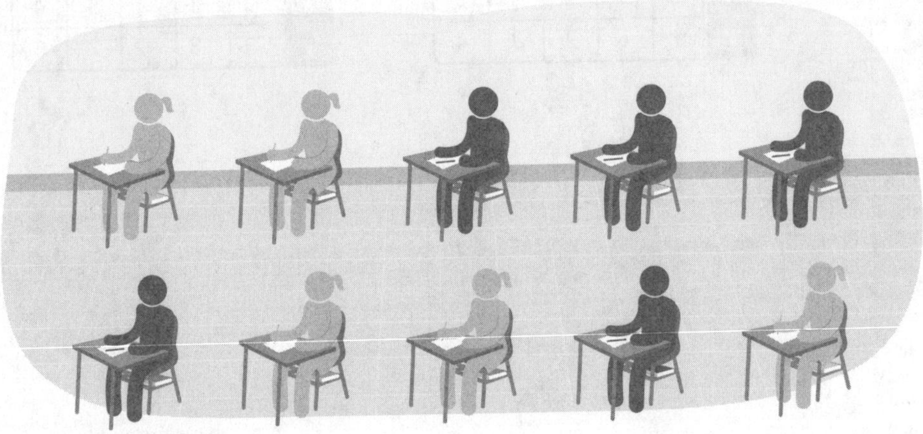

A. What is a reasonable number of rows for the study hall? What is a reasonable number of desks?

B. Look for Structure What number of rows would be impossible? What number of desks would be impossible? Explain.

C. What do your answers to Parts A and B reveal about what the graph of rows to desks looks like?

HABITS OF MIND

Model with Mathematics What other representations could you use to display the student information? Select and describe one representation. Explain how the information would be presented.

Notes

Assess

EXAMPLE 1

Try It! Recognize Domain and Range

1. Identify the domain and the range of each function.

a.

x	2	3	4	5	6
y	0	1	2	3	4

b.

x	−3	−1	1	3	4
y	1	3	−2	2	6

EXAMPLE 2

Try It! Analyze Reasonable Domains and Ranges

2. Analyze each situation. Identify a reasonable domain and range for each situation. Explain.

a. A bowler pays $2.75 per game.

b. A car travels 25 miles using 1 gallon of gas.

HABITS OF MIND

Make Sense and Persevere How do characteristics of a situation impact the domain of a function that describes it?

Assess

EXAMPLE 3

Try It! Classify Relations and Functions

3. Is each relation a function? If so, is it one-to-one or not one-to-one??

a.

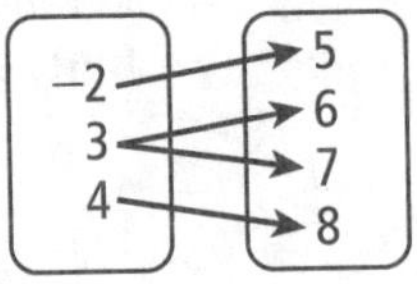

b.

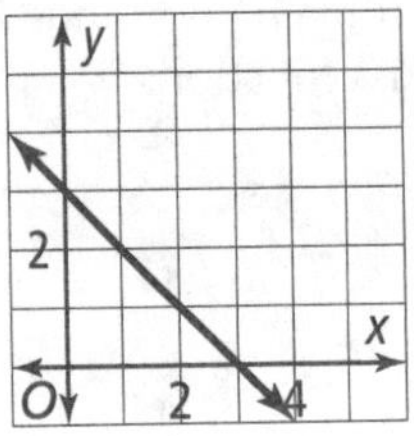

EXAMPLE 4

Try It! Identify Constraints on the Domain

4. Margaret has a monthly clothes budget of \$50. She maps the amount of money she spends each month to the number of items of clothing she buys. What constraints are there on the domain?

HABITS OF MIND

Use Appropriate Tools What are the advantages of using mapping diagrams when analyzing functions? Explain.

Do You UNDERSTAND?

1. ESSENTIAL QUESTION What is a function? Why is domain and range important when defining a function?

2. **Vocabulary** Maya is tracking the amount of rainfall during a storm. Describe the *domain* and *range* for this situation. Include *continuous* or *discrete* in your description.

3. **Reason** What can you conclude about the domain and the range of a function if a vertical line at $x = 5$ passes through 2 points? 1 point? No points? Explain.

4. **Error Analysis** Felipe states that every relation is a function, but not every function is a relation. Explain Felipe's error.

Do You KNOW HOW?

5. Use the graph to determine the domain and range of this relation. Is the relation a function?

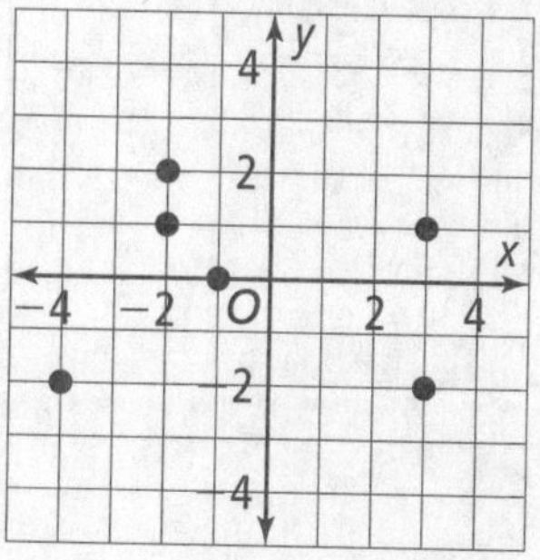

6. For the set of ordered pairs shown, identify the domain and range. Does the relation represent a function?
{(1, 8), (5, 3), (7, 6), (2, 2), (8, 4), (3, 9), (5, 7)}

7. Each day Jacob records the number of laps and the distance he walks, in miles, on a track. Graph the relation and determine whether the distance that Jacob walks is a function of the number of laps.
{(3, 0.75), (6, 1.5), (9, 2.25), (2, 0.5), (7, 1.75), (10, 2.5), (4, 1)}

Activity

3-2 Linear Functions

SavvasRealize.com

MODEL & DISCUSS

The flowchart shows the steps of a math puzzle.

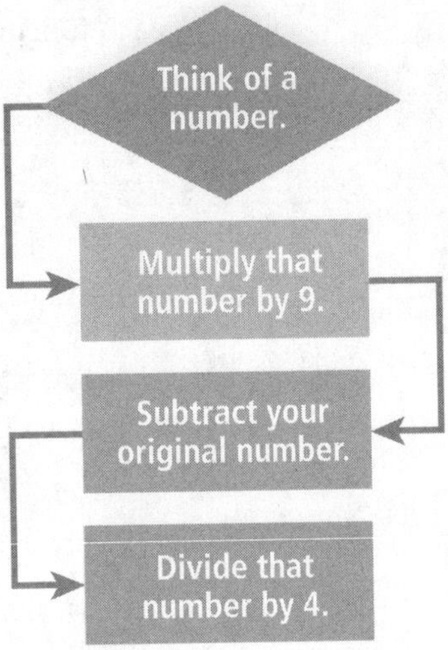

Think of a number.
Multiply that number by 9.
Subtract your original number.
Divide that number by 4.

A. Try the puzzle with 6 different integers.

B. Record each number you try and the result.

C. Make a prediction about what the final number will be for any number. Explain.

D. Use Structure Would your prediction be true for all numbers? Explain.

HABITS OF MIND

Construct Arguments Is it possible to find a counterexample?

Notes

Assess

EXAMPLE 1

Try It! Evaluate Functions in Function Notation

1. Evaluate each function for $x = 4$.

   a. $g(x) = -2x - 3$

   b. $h(x) = 7x + 15$

EXAMPLE 2

Try It! Write a Linear Function Rule

2. Write a linear function for the data in each table using function notation.

a.

x	1	2	3	4
y	6.5	13	19.5	26

b.

x	1	2	3	4
y	1	4	7	10

HABITS OF MIND

Look for Relationships What can the relationship between the values of x and the values of y reveal about a function?

Assess

EXAMPLE 3

Try It! Analyze a Linear Function

3. Sketch the graph of each function.

a. $f(x) = -x + 1$

b. $f(x) = 3x + 1$

EXAMPLE 4

Try It! Use Linear Functions to Solve Problems

4. In Example 4, how would the function, graph, and equation change if the speed is 4 mph? What is the effect on the domain?

HABITS OF MIND

Reason How is a linear function related to a linear equation? Explain.

Do You UNDERSTAND?

1. ESSENTIAL QUESTION How can you identify a linear function?

2. **Communicate Precisely** Give a real-world example of a function that is linear and one that is not linear. Explain.

3. **Vocabulary** What is the difference between a *linear function* and a linear equation?

4. **Error Analysis** The cost of using a game facility is \$1 for every 12 minutes. Talisa writes the function for the cost per hour as $f(x) = 12x$. Explain Talisa's error.

Do You KNOW HOW?

Evaluate each function for $x = 2$ and $x = 6$.

5. $f(x) = 4x - 3$

6. $f(x) = -(x - 2)$

7. Sketch the graph of $f(x) = \frac{1}{2}x + 5$.

8. What function models the height of the periscope lens at time t? If the periscope reaches its maximum height after ascending for 22 seconds, what is the maximum height in feet?

Activity

3-3
Transforming Linear Functions

SavvasRealize.com

CRITIQUE & EXPLAIN

Avery states that the graph of *g* is the same as the graph of *f* with every point shifted vertically. Cindy states that the graph of *g* is the same as the graph of *f* with every point shifted horizontally.

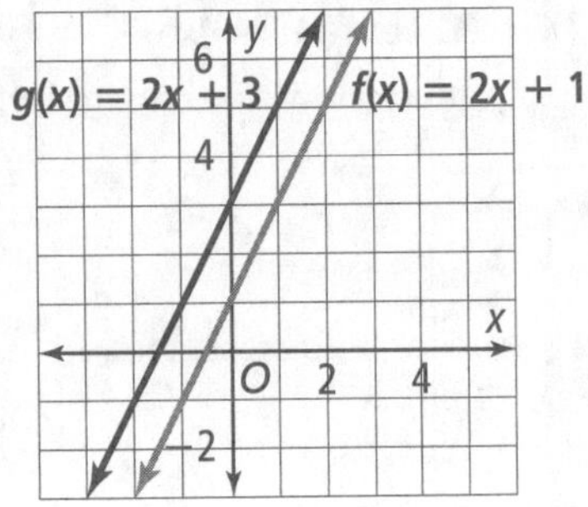

A. Give an argument to support Avery's statement.

B. Give an argument to support Cindy's statement.

C. **Look for Relationships** What do you know about linear equations that might support either of their statements?

HABITS OF MIND

Generalize Would the same arguments apply to the equations of other pairs of parallel lines?

Notes

Assess

EXAMPLE 1

Try It! Vertical Translations of Linear Functions

1. Let $f(x) = -4x$.

   a. How does the graph of $g(x) = -4x - 3$ compare with the graph of f?

   b. How does the graph of $g(x) = -4x + 1.5$ compare with the graph of f?

EXAMPLE 2

Try It! Horizontal Translations of Linear Functions

2. Let $f(x) = 3x + 7$.

   a. How does the graph of $g(x) = 3(x - 4) + 7$ compare with the graph of f?

   b. How does the graph of $g(x) = 3(x + 9.5) + 7$ compare with the graph of f?

HABITS OF MIND

Use Appropriate Tools How does looking at a table of values help you understand translations?

Try It! Stretches and Compressions of Linear Functions

3. Let $f(x) = x - 2$.

   a. How does the graph of $g(x) = 0.25(x - 2)$ compare with the graph of f?

   b. How does the graph of $g(x) = 0.5x - 2$ compare with the graph of f?

HABITS OF MIND

Reason How does the relationship between the elements of the domain and the elements of the range relate to transformations of the function? Explain.

Assess

Do You UNDERSTAND?

1. ESSENTIAL QUESTION How does modifying the input or the output of a linear function rule transform its graph?

2. **Vocabulary** Why is the addition or subtraction of k to the output of a function considered a *translation*?

3. **Error Analysis** The addition or subtraction of a number to a linear a function always moves the line up or down. Describe the error with this reasoning.

4. **Use Structure** Why does multiplying the input of a linear function change only the slope while multiplying the output changes both the slope and the y-intercept?

Do You KNOW HOW?

Given $f(x) = 4x + 1$, describe how the graph of g compares with the graph of f.

5. $g(x) = 4(x + 3) + 1$

6. $g(x) = (4x + 1) + 3$

Given $f(x) = x + 2$, setting $k = 4$ affects the slope and y-intercept of the graph of g compared to the graph of f.

7. $g(x) = 4(x + 2)$

8. $g(x) = (4x) + 2$

9. The minimum wage for employees of a company is modeled by the function $f(x) = 7.25$. The company decided to offer a signing bonus of \$75. How does adding this amount affect a graph of an employee's earnings?

Video

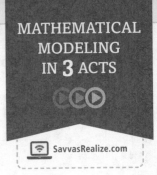

MATHEMATICAL MODELING IN 3 ACTS

SavvasRealize.com

The Express Lane

Some supermarkets have self checkout lanes. Customers scan their items themselves and then pay with either cash or credit when they have finished scanning all of the items. Some customers think these lanes are faster than the checkout lanes with cashiers, but others don't like having to bag all of their purchases themselves.

What's your strategy for picking a checkout lane at the grocery store? Think about this during the Mathematical Modeling in 3 Acts lesson.

ACT 1 Identify the Problem

1. What is the first question that comes to mind after watching the video?

2. Write down the main question you will answer about what you saw in the video.

3. Make an initial conjecture that answers this main question.

4. Explain how you arrived at your conjecture.

5. What information will be useful to know to answer the main question? How can you get it? How will you use that information?

ACT 2 Develop a Model

6. Use the math that you have learned in the topic to refine your conjecture.

ACT 3 Interpret the Results

7. Did your refined conjecture match the actual answer exactly? If not, what might explain the difference?

Activity

3-4 Arithmetic Sequences

SavvasRealize.com

EXPLORE & REASON

A fashion designer is designing a patterned fabric.

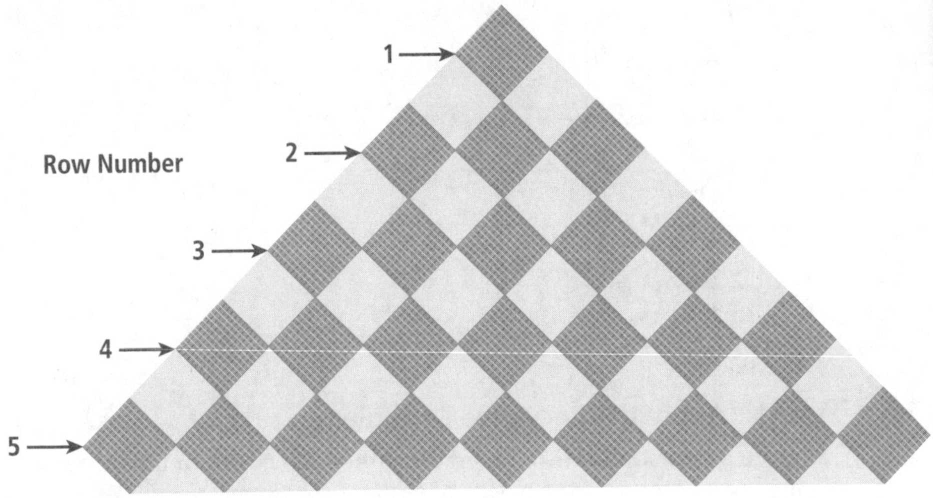

A. Copy and complete.

Row number	1	2	3	4	5
Number of Patterned Squares in the Row	1	■	5	■	■
Total Number of Patterned Squares	1	■	9	■	■

B. Use Structure What number patterns do you see in the rows of the table?

HABITS OF MIND

Model with Mathematics What information would you need from the table to write a linear equation that represents the pattern? Explain.

Notes

Assess

EXAMPLE 1

Try It! Connect Sequences and Functions

1. Is the domain of the function in Part B of Example 1 continuous or discrete? Explain.

EXAMPLE 2

Try It! Apply the Recursive Formula

2. Write a recursive formula to represent the total height of the nth stair above the ground if the height of each stair is 18 cm.

EXAMPLE 3

Try It! Apply the Explicit Formula

3. The cost to rent a bike is $28 for the first day plus $2 for each day after that. Write an explicit formula for the rental cost for n days. What is the cost of renting the bike for 8 days?

HABITS OF MIND

Reason Can a recursive formula have a negative common difference? Explain.

Assess

EXAMPLE 4

Try It! Write an Explicit Formula From a Recursive Formula

4. Write an explicit formula for each arithmetic sequence.

a. $a_n = a_{n-1} - 3$; $a_1 = 10$

b. $a_n = a_{n-1} + 2.4$; $a_1 = -1$

EXAMPLE 5

Try It! Write a Recursive Formula From an Explicit Formula

5. Write a recursive formula for each explicit formula.

a. $a_n = 8 + 3n$

b. $a_n = 12 - 5n$

HABITS OF MIND

Communicate Precisely Explain how you can use the recursive formula to find the value of any term in an arithmetic sequence.

Assess

Do You UNDERSTAND?

1. ESSENTIAL QUESTION How are arithmetic sequences related to linear functions?

2. **Error Analysis** A student uses the explicit formula $a_n = 5 + 3(n - 1)$ for the sequence 3, 8, 13, 18, 23, ... to find the 12th term. Explain the error the student made.

3. **Vocabulary** When is a *recursive formula* more useful than an *explicit formula* for an arithmetic sequence?

4. **Communicate Precisely** Compare and contrast a recursive formula and an explicit formula for an arithmetic sequence.

Do You KNOW HOW?

Tell whether or not each sequence is an arithmetic sequence.

5. 15, 13, 11, 9, . . .

6. 4, 7, 10, 14, . . .

Write a recursive formula for each sequence.

7. 81, 85, 89, 93, 97, . . .

8. 47, 39, 31, 23, 15, . . .

9. An online store charges $5 to ship one box and $10 to ship two boxes. Write an explicit formula for an arithmetic sequence to represent the amount the online store charges to ship *n* boxes. Use the explicit formula to determine how much the online store charges when shipping 11 boxes.

3-5 Scatter Plots and Lines of Fit

MODEL & DISCUSS

Nicholas plotted data points to represent the relationship between screen size and cost of television sets. Everything about the televisions is the same, except for the screen size.

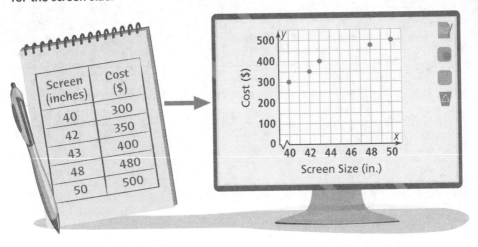

Screen (inches)	Cost ($)
40	300
42	350
43	400
48	480
50	500

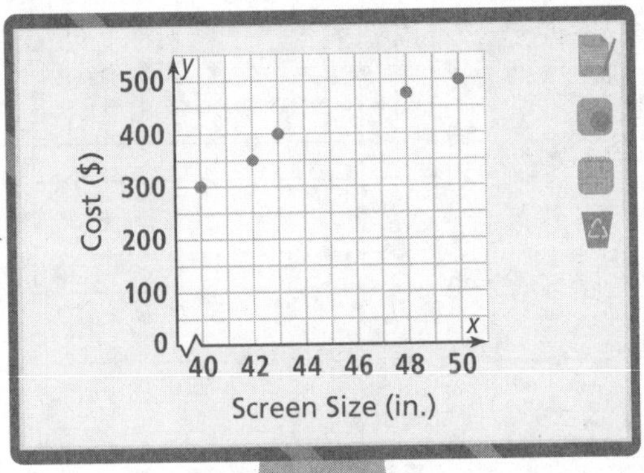

A. Describe any patterns you see.

B. What does this set of points tell you about the relationship of screen size and cost of the television?

C. Reason Where do you think the point for a 46-inch television would be on the graph? How about for a 60-inch TV? Explain.

HABITS OF MIND

Use Appropriate Tools How can a table of values help determine whether data can be modeled by a linear function?

Notes

EXAMPLE 1

Try It! Understand Association

1. Describe the type of association each scatter plot shows.

a.

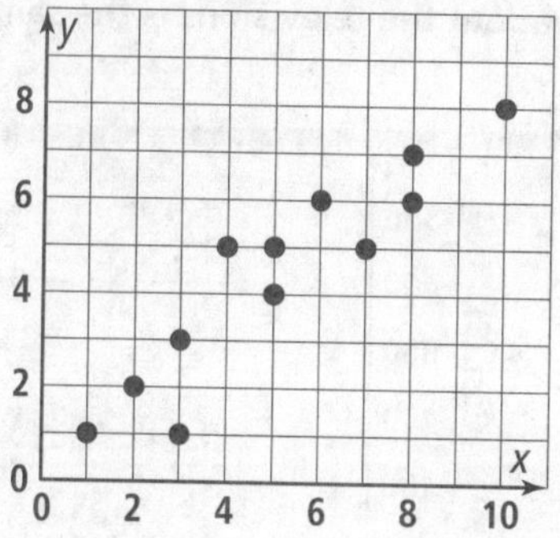

b.

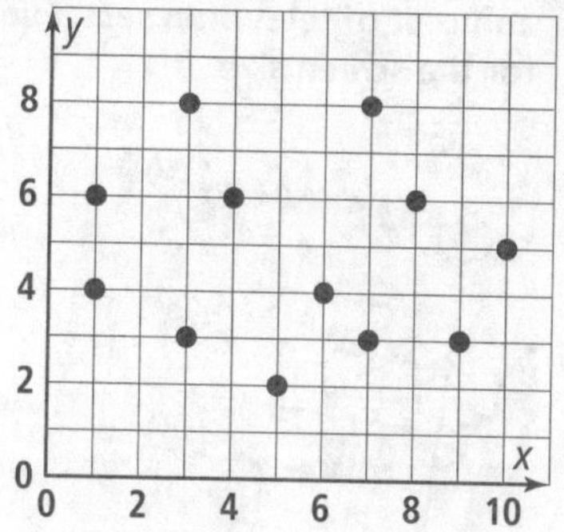

HABITS OF MIND

Reason What features of two data sets can help you determine whether the data sets have a negative, positive, or no association?

EXAMPLE 2

Try It! Understand Correlation

2. How can the relationship between the hours after sunset x and the temperature y be modeled? If the relationship is modeled with a linear function, describe the correlation between the two data sets.

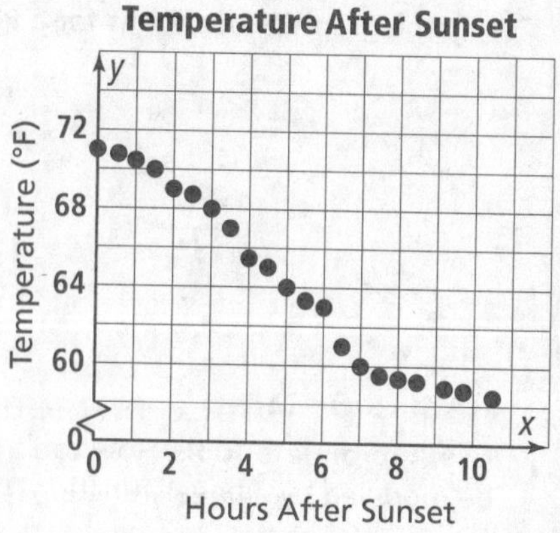

Notes

Assess

EXAMPLE 3

Try It! Write the Equation of a Trend Line

3. a. What trend line, in slope-intercept form, models the data from the Example 2 Try It?

b. Explain why there could be no data points on a trend line, yet the line models the data.

EXAMPLE 4

Try It! Interpret Trend Lines

4. What is the x-intercept of the trend line? Is that possible in a real-world situation? Explain.

HABITS OF MIND

Construct Arguments What argument can you construct to defend a prediction based on a trend line? Explain.

Do You UNDERSTAND?

1. ESSENTIAL QUESTION How can you use a scatter plot to describe the relationship between two data sets?

2. **Error Analysis** A student claims that if y-values are not increasing as x-values increase, then the data must show a negative association. Explain the error the student made.

3. **Vocabulary** In a scatter plot that shows *positive association*, describe how y-values change as x-values increase

4. **Make Sense and Persevere** Does a trend line need to pass through all the points in a scatter plot? Explain.

5. **Communicate Precisely** Describe how the point-slope formula is useful when writing the equation for a trend line.

Do You KNOW HOW?

Describe the type of association between x and y for each set of data. Explain.

6.

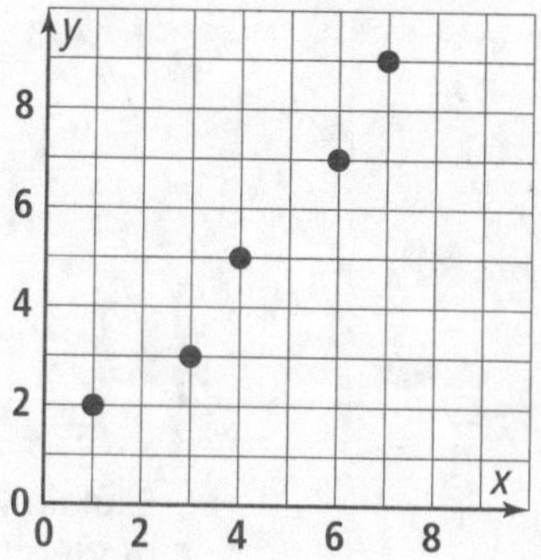

7.

x	4	6	7	9	10
y	9	7	5	3	3

8. The table shows the hours of studying x and a person's test score y. What is the equation of a trend line that models the data? What does the slope of your trend line represent?

Hours of Studying	0	1	1	2	3
Test Score	77	80	83	87	92

Activity

3-6 Analyzing Lines of Fit

SavvasRealize.com

MODEL & DISCUSS

The scatter plot shows the number of beachgoers each day for the first six days of July. The head lifeguard at the beach uses the data to determine the number of lifeguards to schedule based on the weather forecast.

The head lifeguard compares two linear models:

$g(x) = 13x + 25$

$h(x) = 12x + 30$

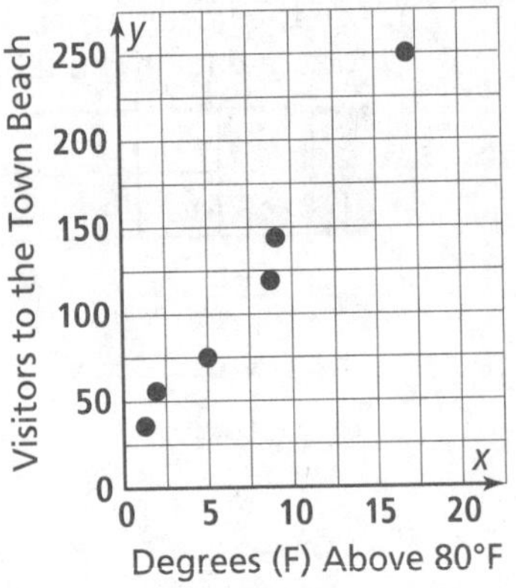

A. Copy the scatter plot and graph the linear functions on the same grid.

B. What is a reasonable domain for each function? Explain.

C. Construct Arguments Which model is the better predictor of the number of beachgoers based on the temperature above 80°F? Defend your model.

HABITS OF MIND

Generalize Is there a limit to the number of lines that might be used to fit a set of points on a graph? Explain.

Notes

Assess

EXAMPLE 1 **Try It!** **Find the Line of Best Fit**

1. Use the linear regression function to find the equation of the line of best fit for the data in the table.

x	1	2	4	5	7	8	9
y	5.4	6.1	8.1	8.5	10.3	10.9	11.5

EXAMPLE 2 **Try It!** **Understand Correlation Coefficients**

2. What does each correlation coefficient reveal about the data it describes?

a. $r = 0.1$

b. $r = -0.6$

HABITS OF MIND

Communicate Precisely How are a strong negative correlation and a weak correlation different? Explain.

Assess

EXAMPLE 3

Try It! Interpret Residual Plots

3. The owner of Horizon Flight School also created a scatter plot and calculated the line of best fit for her enrollment data shown in the table. The equation of the line of best fit is $y = 1.44x + 877$. Find the residuals and plot them to determine how well this linear model fits the data.

Year (x)	0	1	2	3	4	5	6	7
Students (y)	832	872	905	928	903	887	863	867

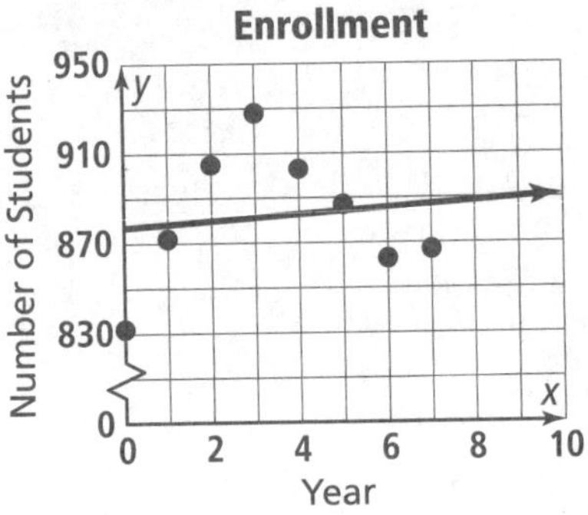

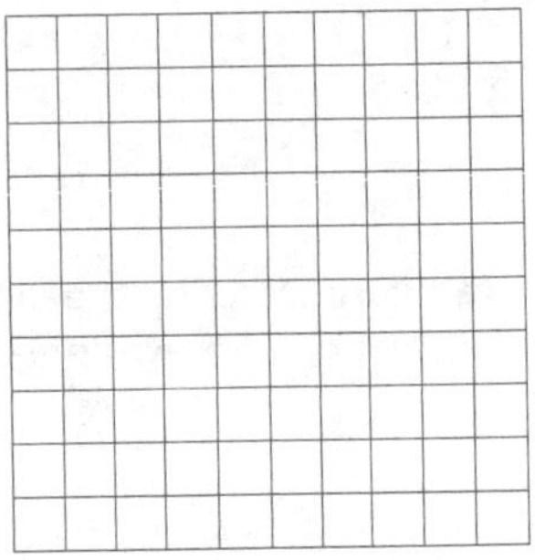

EXAMPLE 4

Try It! Interpolate and Extrapolate Using Linear Models

4. Using the model from Example 4, estimate the number of miles people flew on the airline in 2012.

EXAMPLE 5

Try It! Correlation and Causation

5. The number of cars in a number of cities shows a positive correlation to the population of the respective city. Can it be inferred that an increase of cars in a city leads to an increase in the population? Defend your response.

HABITS OF MIND

Construct Arguments What argument can you construct to explain why a given relationship would not be causal? Explain.

Do You UNDERSTAND?

1. **ESSENTIAL QUESTION** How can you evaluate the goodness of fit of a line of best fit for a paired data set?

2. **Vocabulary** Describe the difference between *interpolation* and *extrapolation*.

3. **Error Analysis** A student says that a correlation coefficient of −0.93 indicates that the two quantities of a data set have a weak correlation. Explain the error the student made.

4. **Look for Relationships** A student found a strong correlation between the age of people who run marathons and their marathon time. Can the student say that young people will run marathons faster than older people? Explain.

Do You KNOW HOW?

Use the table for Exercises 5 and 6.

x	10	20	30	40	50
y	7	11	14	20	22

5. Use technology to determine the equation of the line of best fit for the data.

6. Make a residual plot for the line of best fit and the data in the table. How well does the linear model fit the data?

7. The table shows the number of customers y at a store for x weeks after the store's grand opening. The equation for the line of best fit is $y = 7.77x + 38.8$. Assuming the trend continues, what is a reasonable prediction of the number of visitors to the store 7 weeks after its opening?

x	1	2	3	4	5	6
y	46	53	65	71	75	86

Activity

4-1

Solving Systems of Equations by Graphing

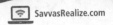

SavvasRealize.com

EXPLORE & REASON

Juan and Leo were supposed to meet and drive ATVs on a trail together. Juan is late so Leo started without him.

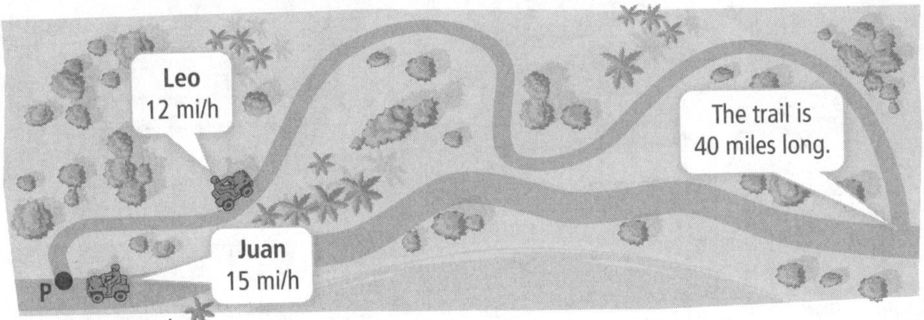

Not drawn to scale

A. Write an equation for Leo's distance from the starting point after riding for x hours. Write an equation for Juan's distance from the starting point if he starts h hours after Leo.

B. **Model With Mathematics** Suppose $h = 1$. How can you use graphs of the two equations to determine who finishes the trail first?

C. How much of a head start must Leo have to finish the trail at the same time as Juan?

HABITS OF MIND

Make Sense and Persevere Suppose Leo got a 10-mile head start. About how long would he be waiting at the end of the trail before Juan got there?

Notes

Assess

EXAMPLE 1

Try It! Solve a System of Equations by Graphing

1. Use a graph to solve each system of equations.

a. $\begin{cases} y = \frac{1}{2}x - 2 \\ y = 3x - 7 \end{cases}$

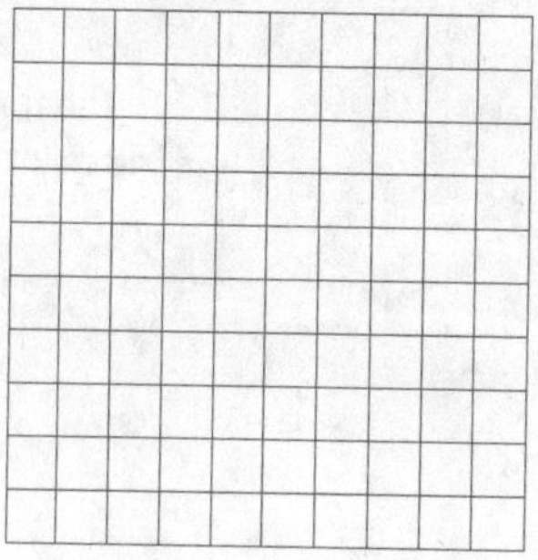

b. $\begin{cases} y = 2x + 10 \\ y = -\frac{1}{4}x + 1 \end{cases}$

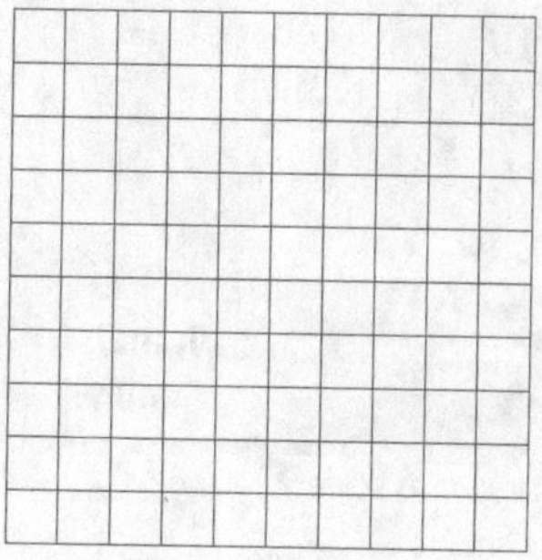

EXAMPLE 2

Try It! Graph Systems of Equations With Infinitely Many or No Solutions

2. Use a graph to solve each system of equations.

a. $\begin{cases} y = \frac{1}{2}x + 7 \\ 4x - 8y = 12 \end{cases}$

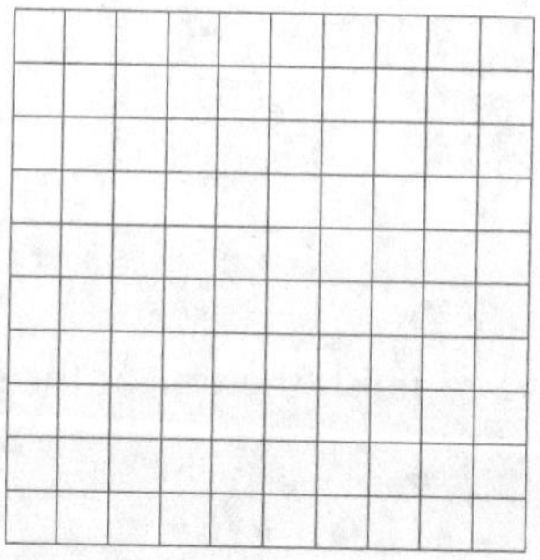

b. $\begin{cases} 3x + 2y = 9 \\ \frac{2}{3}y = 3 - x \end{cases}$

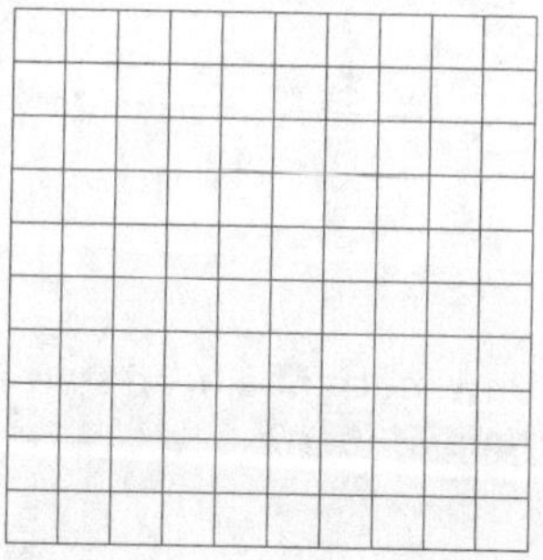

HABITS OF MIND

Reason Other than graphing, how else could you determine that an equation has infinitely many solutions?

EXAMPLE 3

Try It! Write a System of Equations

3. Suppose Monisha reads 10 pages each day instead.
   a. How will that change the length of time it takes for Holly to catch up with Monisha?

   b. Will Holly still finish the novel first? Explain.

EXAMPLE 4

Try It! Solve a System of Equations Approximately

4. What solution do you obtain for the system of equations by graphing? What is the exact solution?

   $y = 5x - 4$
   $y = -6x + 14$

HABITS OF MIND

Use Appropriate Tools Holly and Monisha's classmate, Chris, is also finishing the novel. Chris has read 64 pages of the novel and plans to read 13 pages each day. When does Holly catch up to Chris? Does Chris finish the novel before Monisha?

Do You UNDERSTAND?

1. ESSENTIAL QUESTION How can you use a graph to illustrate the solution to a system of linear equations?

2. **Model With Mathematics** How does the graph of a system of equations with one solution differ from the graph of a system of equations with infinitely many solutions or no solution?

3. **Reason** Why is the point of intersection for a system of equations considered its solution?

4. **Error Analysis** Reese states that the system of equations has no solution because the slopes are the same. Describe Reese's error.

$$y = -3x - 1$$
$$3x + y = -1$$

Do You KNOW HOW?

Solve each system of equations by graphing.

5. $y = 2x + 5$
$y = -\frac{1}{2}x$

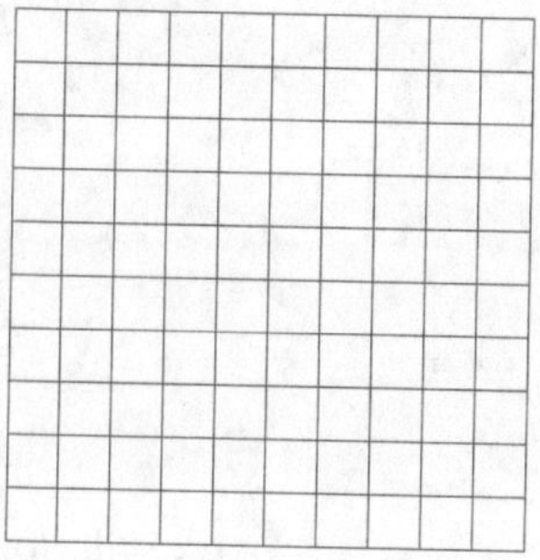

6. $y = -\frac{2}{3}x + 2$
$2x + 3y = 6$

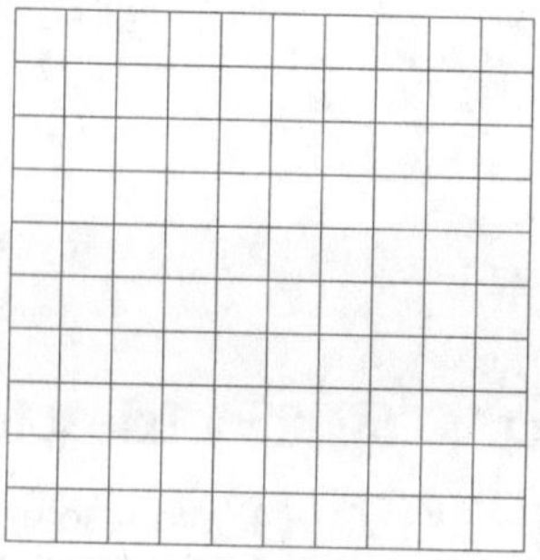

7. Juanita is painting her house. She can either buy Brand A paint and a paint roller tray or Brand B paint and a grid for the paint roller. For how many gallons of paint would the price for both options be the same? If Juanita needs 15 gallons of paint, which is the better option?

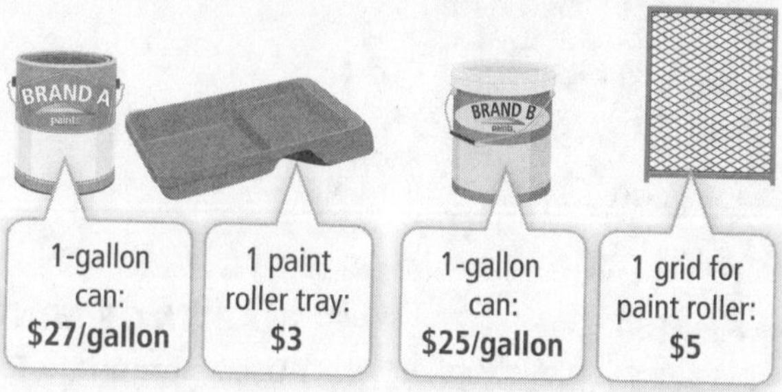

Activity

4-2 Solving Systems of Equations by Substitution

SavvasRealize.com

MODEL & DISCUSS

Rochelle is conducting an experiment on cells of Elodea, a kind of water plant. To induce plasmolysis at the correct rate, she needs to use an 8% saline solution but she has only the solutions shown on hand.

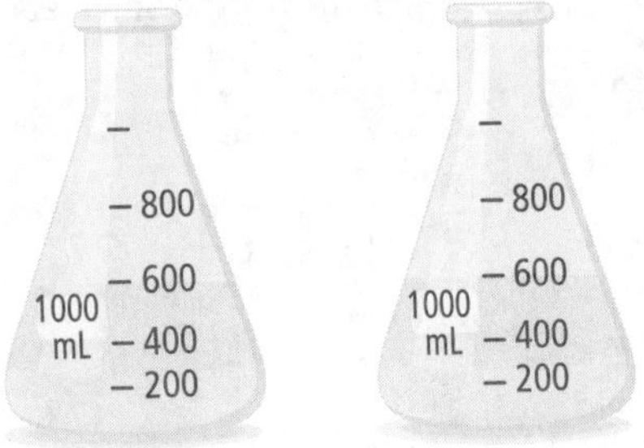

Solution A 10% saline

Solution B 5% saline

A. If Rochelle mixes the two solutions to get 1,000 mL of an 8% saline solution, which will she use more of? Explain.

B. How can Rochelle determine the amount of each solution she needs to make the 8% saline solution?

C. **Use Appropriate Tools** Are there any methods for solving this problem other than the one you used in part (b)? Explain.

HABITS OF MIND

Look for Relationships Next, Rochelle wants to make 1,000 mL of a 7% saline solution. Would the amount of 10% solution in the 7% saline solution be more or less than the amount in the 8% saline solution? Explain.

Notes

Assess

EXAMPLE 1

Try It! Solve Systems of Equations Using Substitution

1. Use substitution to solve each system of equations.

   a. $x = y + 6$
      $x + y = 10$

   b. $y = 2x - 1$
      $2x + 3y = -7$

EXAMPLE 2

Try It! Compare Graphing and Substitution Methods

2. On Saturday, the vacation resort offers a discount on water sports. To take a surfing lesson and go parasailing costs $130. That day, 25 people take surfing lessons, and 30 people go parasailing. A total of $3,650 is collected. What is the discounted price of each activity?

HABITS OF MIND

Generalize If you visit the vacation resort and find the cost of surfing lessons and parasailing by graphing the system of equations, what will you need to remember about the solution that you find?

Notes

Assess

EXAMPLE 3

Try It! Systems With Infinitely Many Solutions or No Solution

3. Solve each system of equations.

a. $x + y = -4$
$y = -x + 5$

b. $y = -2x + 5$
$2x + y = 5$

EXAMPLE 4

Try It! Model Using Systems of Equations

4. Funtime Amusement Park charges \$12.50 for admission and then \$0.75 per ride. River's Edge Park charges \$18.50 for admission and then \$0.50 per ride. For what number of rides is the cost the same at both parks?

HABITS OF MIND

Make Sense and Persevere Healthy Start gym charges \$32 for membership and then \$6 per cycling class. Fast Fitness charges \$29 for membership and then \$6 per cycling class. Does a number of cycling classes exist for which the cost is the same at both gyms?

Assess

Do You UNDERSTAND?

1. ESSENTIAL QUESTION How do you use substitution to solve a system of linear equations?

2. **Use Appropriate Tools** When is using a graph to solve a system of equations more useful than the substitution method?

3. **Error Analysis** Simon solves a system of equations, in x and y, by substitution and gets an answer of $5 = 5$. He states that the solution to the system is all of the points (x, y) where x and y are real numbers. Describe Simon's error.

4. **Use Structure** When solving a system of equations using substitution, how can you determine whether the system has one solution, no solution, or infinitely many solutions?

Do You KNOW HOW?

Use substitution to solve each system of equations.

5. $y = 6 - x$
   $4x - 3y = -4$

6. $x = -y + 3$
   $3x - 2y = -1$

7. $-3x - y = 7$
   $x + 2y = 6$

8. $6x - 3y = -6$
   $y = 2x + 2$

9. A sports store sells a total of 70 soccer balls in one month, and collects a total of $2,400. Write and solve a system of equations to determine how many of each type of soccer ball were sold.

Activity

CRITIQUE & EXPLAIN

Sadie and Micah used different methods to solve the system of equations.

$$y = 2x + 3$$
$$4x - y = 5$$

Sadie's work

$4x - (2x + 3) = 5$
$4x - 2x - 3 = 5$
$2x - 3 = 5$
$2x = 8$
$x = 4$
$y = 2(4) + 3 = 11$
The solution is (4, 11).

Micah's work

$y = 2x + 3$ and $y = 4x - 5$
$2x + 3 = 4x - 5$
$8 = 2x$
$x = 4$
$y = 2(4) + 3$
$y = 11$
The solution is (4, 11).

A. In what ways are Sadie's and Micah's approaches similar? In what ways are they different?

B. Are both Sadie's and Micah's approaches valid solution methods? Explain.

C. Reason Which method of solving systems of equations do you prefer when solving, Sadie's method, or Micah's method? Explain.

HABITS OF MIND

Reason Can you think of an instance when it is more convenient to use Sadie's method? When is it more convenient to use Micah's method?

4-3 Solving Systems of Equations by Elimination

SavvasRealize.com

Notes

Assess

EXAMPLE 1

Try It! Solve a System of Equations by Adding

1. Solve each system of equations.

a. $2x - 4y = 2$
$-x + 4y = 3$

b. $2x + 3y = 1$
$-2x + 2y = -6$

EXAMPLE 2

Try It! Understand Equivalent Systems of Equations

2. Solve each system of equations.

a. $x + 2y = 4$
$2x - 5y = -1$

b. $2x + y = 2$
$x - 2y = -5$

HABITS OF MIND

Look for Relationships How could you write an equivalent system of equations for both of the systems in Try It! 2?

EXAMPLE 3

Try It! Apply Elimination

3. Before the florist has a chance to finish the bouquets, a large order is placed. After the order, only 85 roses and 163 peonies remain. How many regular bouquets and mini bouquets can the florist make now?

EXAMPLE 4

Try It! Choose a Method of Solving

4. What is the solution of each system of equations? Explain your choice of solution method.

   a. $6x + 12y = -6$
      $3x - 2y = -27$

   b. $3x - 2y = 38$
      $x = 6 - y$

HABITS OF MIND

Communicate Precisely Explain the difference between solving a system of equations using substitution and solving a system of equations using elimination.

Assess

Do You UNDERSTAND?

1. ESSENTIAL QUESTION Why does the elimination method work when solving a system of equations?

2. **Error Analysis** Esteban tries to solve the following system.

$$7x - 4y = -12$$
$$x - 2y = 4$$

His first step is to multiply the second equation by 3.

$$7x - 4y = -12$$
$$3x - 6y = 12$$

Then he adds the equations to eliminate a term. What is Esteban's error?

3. **Construct Arguments** How can you determine whether two systems of equations are equivalent?

4. **Mathematical Connections** The sum of 5 times the width of a rectangle and twice its length is 26 units. The difference of 15 times the width and three times the length is 6 units. Write and solve a system of equations to find the length and width of the rectangle.

Do You KNOW HOW?

Solve each system of equations.

5. $4x - 2y = -2$
$3x + 2y = -12$

6. $3x + 2y = 4$
$3x + 6y = -24$

7. $4x - 3y = -9$
$3x + 2y = -11$

8. $x - 3y = -4$
$2x - 6y = 6$

9. Ella is a landscape photographer. One weekend at her gallery she sells a total of 52 prints for a total of \$2,975. How many of each size print did Ella sell?

Small print: \$50

Large print: \$75

Activity

4-4 Linear Inequalities in Two Variables

SavvasRealize.com

MODEL & DISCUSS

A flatbed trailer carrying a load can have a maximum total height of 13 feet, 6 inches. The photograph shows the height of the trailer before a load is placed on top. What are the possible heights of loads that could be carried on the trailer?

A. What type of model could represent this situation? Explain.

B. Will the type of model you chose show all the possible heights of the loads without going over the maximum height? Explain.

C. Reason Interpret the solutions of the model. How many solutions are there? Explain.

HABITS OF MIND

Make Sense and Persevere Suppose that the maximum load is transferred to a different flat bed. If the new flat bed has a maximum total height of 14 feet, what should the height of the new load on the flatbed be to ensure the flatbed and the load do not exceed the maximum total height?

Notes

Assess

EXAMPLE 1

Try It! Understand an Inequality in Two Variables

1. Describe the graph of the solutions of each inequality.

   a. $y < -3x + 5$.

   b. $y \geq -3x + 5$

EXAMPLE 2

Try It! Rewrite an Inequality to Graph It

2. Will the Science Club meet their goal if they sell 30 T-shirts and 90 key chains? Explain in terms of the graph of the inequality.

HABITS OF MIND

Communicate Precisely How is the graph of $y < 3x$ similar to the graph of $y \geq 3x$? How are the two graphs different?

EXAMPLE 3

Try It! Write an Inequality From a Graph

3. What inequality does each graph represent?

a.

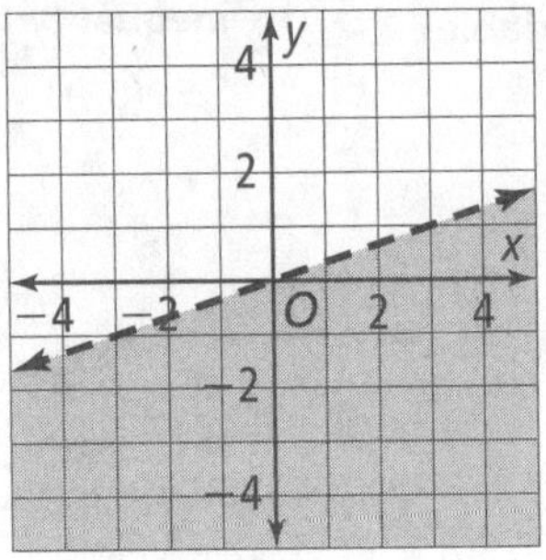

b.

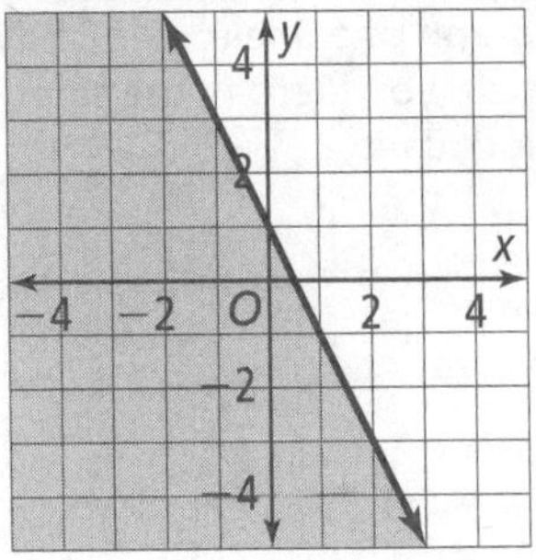

EXAMPLE 4

Try It! Inequalities in One Variable in the Coordinate Plane

4. Graph each inequality in the coordinate plane.

a. $y > -2$

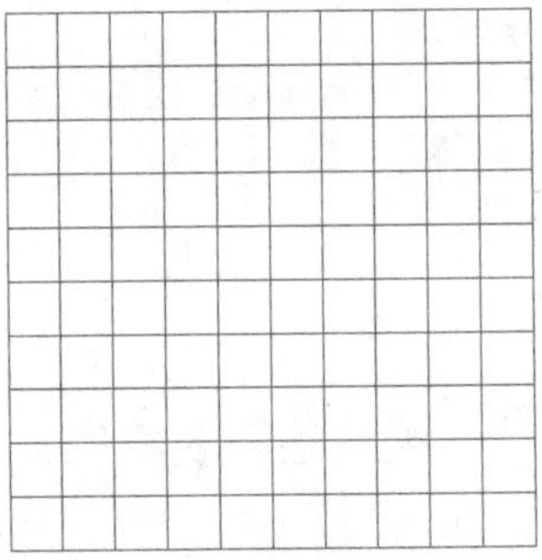

b. $x \leq 1$

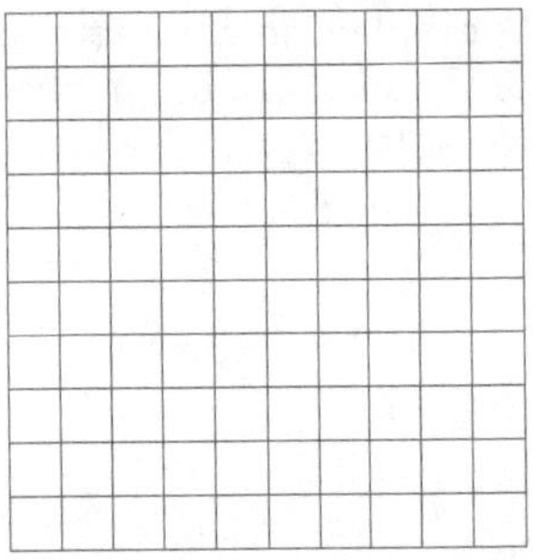

HABITS OF MIND

Use Appropriate Tools Name two ways you could check if a point is a solution of an inequality.

Do You UNDERSTAND?

1. ESSENTIAL QUESTION How does the graph of a linear inequality in two variables help you identify the solutions of the inequality?

2. **Communicate Precisely** How many solutions does a linear inequality in two variables have?

3. **Vocabulary** In what form do you write one of the *solutions of an inequality in two variables*?

4. **Error Analysis** A student claims that the inequality $y < 1$ cannot be graphed on a coordinate grid since it has only one variable. Explain the error the student made.

Do You KNOW HOW?

Tell whether each ordered pair is a solution of the inequality $y > x + 1$.

5. (0, 1)

6. (3, 5)

Graph each inequality in the coordinate plane.

7. $y \geq 2x$

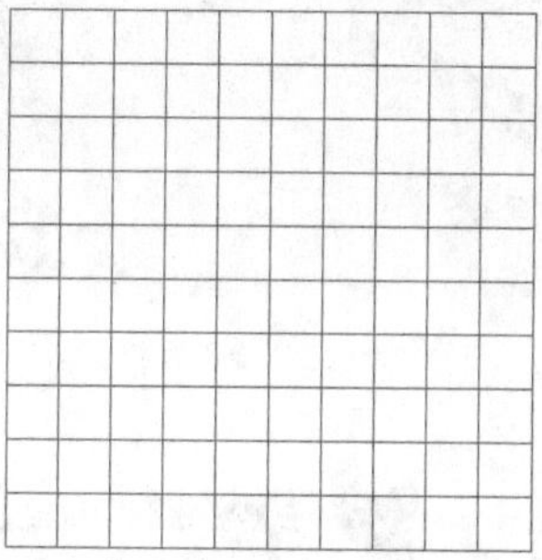

8. $y < x - 2$

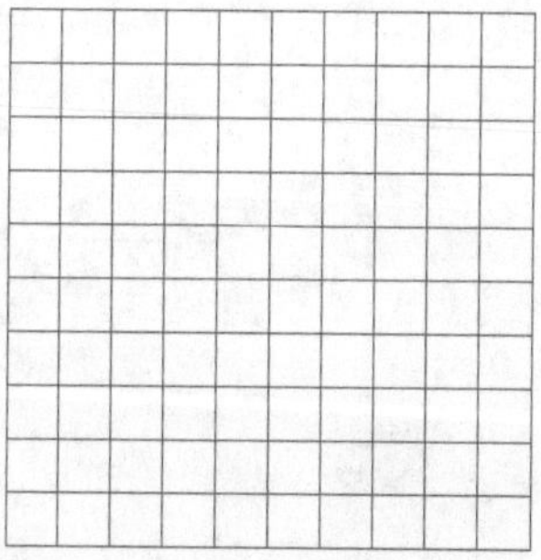

9. What inequality is shown by the graph?

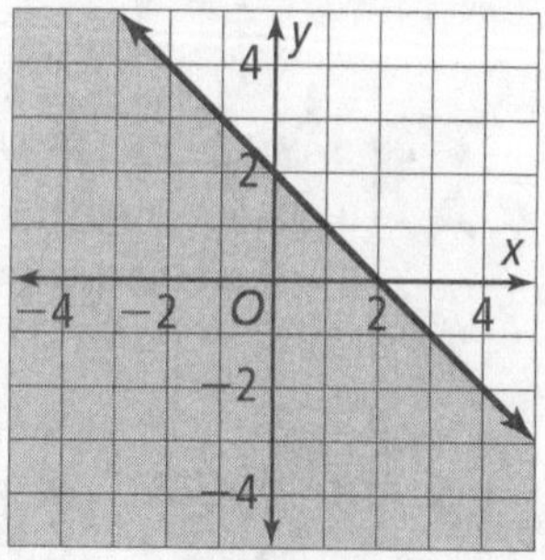

Video

MATHEMATICAL MODELING IN 3 ACTS

SavvasRealize.com

Get Up There!

Have you ever been to the top of a skyscraper? If so, you probably didn't take the stairs. You probably took an elevator. How long did it take you to get to the top? Did you take an express elevator?

Express elevators travel more quickly because they do not stop at every floor. How much more quickly can you get to the top in an express elevator? Think about this during the Mathematical Modeling in 3 Acts lesson.

ACT 1

1. What is the first question that comes to mind after watching the video?

2. Write down the main question you will answer about what you saw in the video.

3. Make an initial conjecture that answers this main question.

4. Explain how you arrived at your conjecture.

5. What information will be useful to know to answer the main question? How can you get it? How will you use that information?

ACT 2

6. Use the math that you have learned in the topic to refine your conjecture.

ACT 3

7. Did your refined conjecture match the actual answer exactly? If not, what might explain the difference?

Activity

4-5 Systems of Linear Inequalities

SavvasRealize.com

EXPLORE & REASON

The graph shows the equations $y = x - 1$ and $y = -2x + 4$.

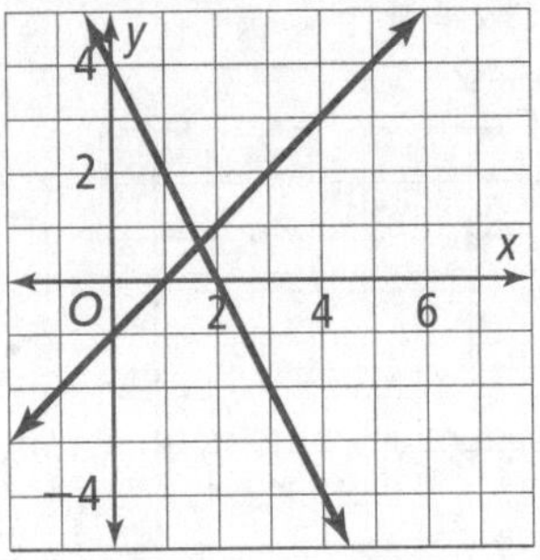

A. Choose some points above and below the line $y = x - 1$. Which of them are solutions to $y > x - 1$? Which are solutions to $y < x - 1$?

B. Choose some points above and below the line $y = -2x + 4$. Which of them are solutions to $y > -2x + 4$? Which are solutions to $y < -2x + 4$?

C. Look for Relationships The two lines divide the plane into four regions. How can you describe each region in terms of the inequalities in parts A and B?

HABITS OF MIND

Reason Are points on the line part of any of the four regions described in Part C? Explain.

Notes

Assess

EXAMPLE 1

Try It! Graph a System of Inequalities

1. Graph each system of inequalities.

a. $y < 2x$
$y > -3$

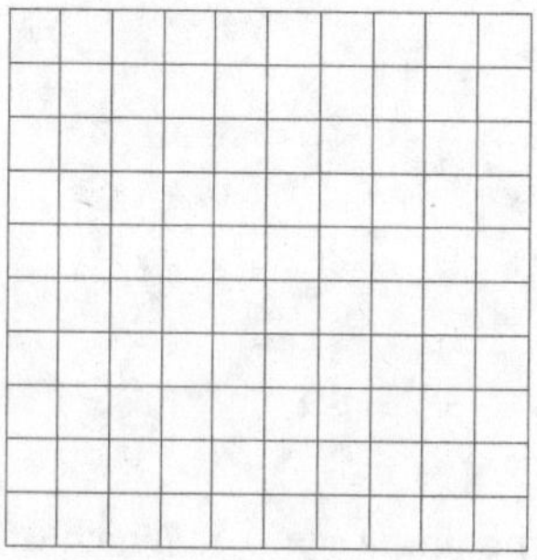

b. $y \geq -2x + 1$
$y > x + 2$

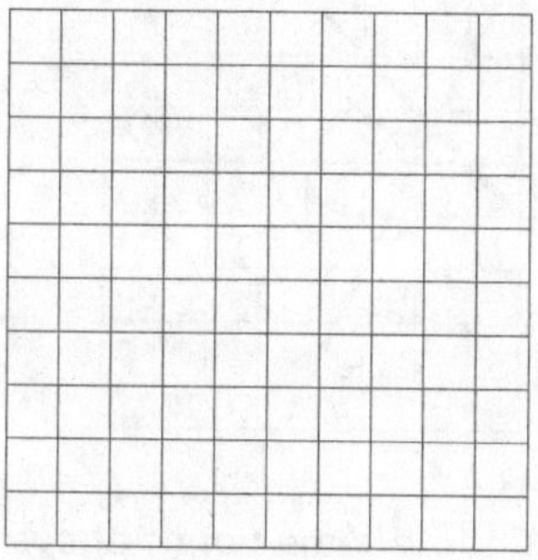

EXAMPLE 2

Try It! Write a System of Inequalities From a Graph

2. What system of inequalities is shown by each graph?

a.

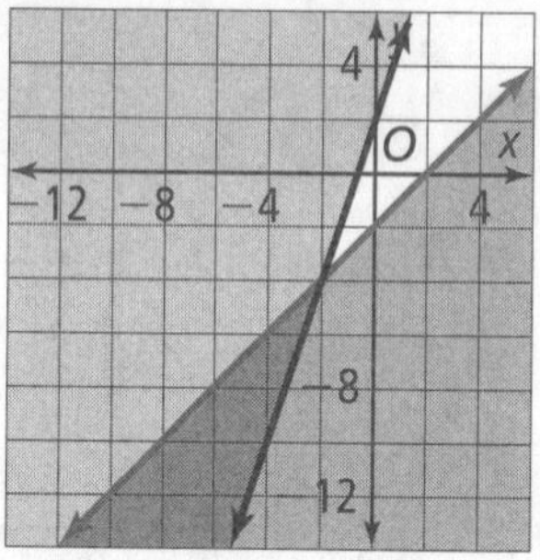

b.

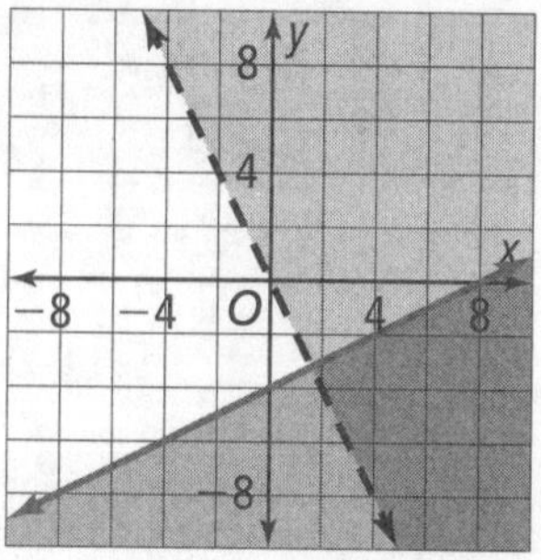

HABITS OF MIND

Use Appropriate Tools What would the graph of a system of inequalities with no solutions look like?

Notes

Assess

EXAMPLE 3

Try It! Use a System of Inequalities

3. Use the graph in Example 3 to determine if Malia can buy 75 water bottles and 100 pairs of socks. Explain.

HABITS OF MIND

Generalize What do the nonoverlapping portions of the shaded regions represent?

Do You UNDERSTAND?

1. **ESSENTIAL QUESTION** How is the graph of a system of linear inequalities related to the solutions of the system of inequalities?

2. **Error Analysis** A student say that (0, 1) is a solution to the following system of inequalities.

   $y > x$
   $y > 2x + 1$

   She says that (0, 1) is a solution because it is a solution of $y > x$. Explain the error that the student made.

3. **Vocabulary** How many inequalities are in a *system of inequalities*?

4. **Use Appropriate Tools** Is it easier to describe the solution of a system of linear inequalities in words or to show it using a graph? Explain.

Do You KNOW HOW?

Identify the boundary lines for each system of inequalities.

5. $y > -3x + 4$
   $y \leq 8x + 1$

6. $y < -6x$
   $y \geq 10x - 3$

Graph each system of inequalities.

7. $y \leq -3x$
   $y < 2$

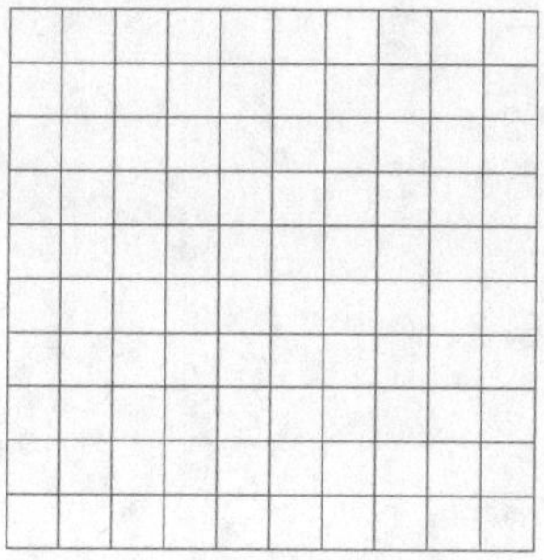

8. $y \geq x - 4$
   $y < -x$

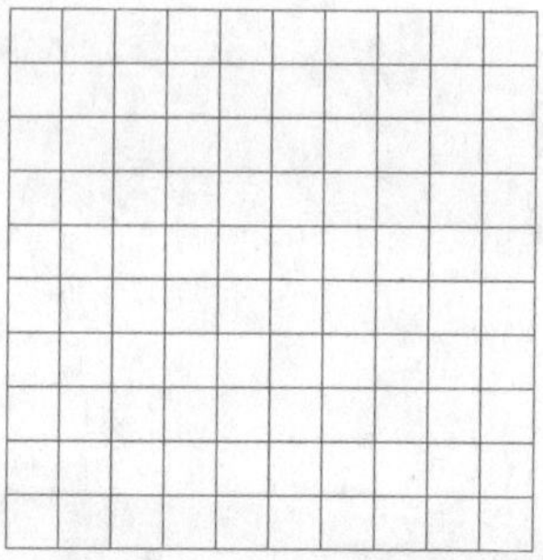

9. What system of inequalities is shown by the graph?

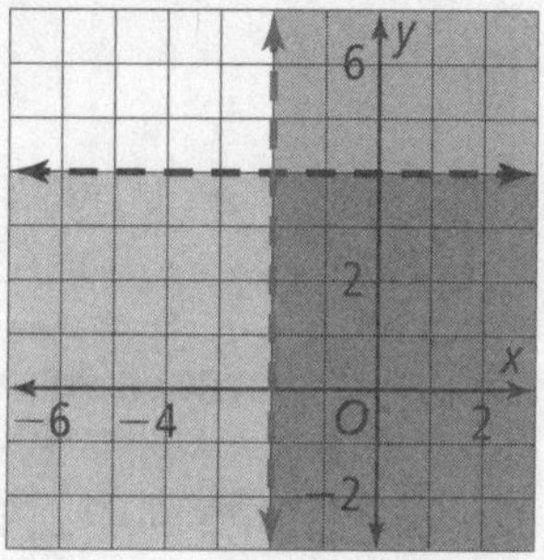

Activity

CRITIQUE & EXPLAIN

Students are asked to write an equivalent expression for 3^{-3}. Casey and Jacinta each write an expression on the board.

Casey	Jacinta
$3^{-3} = -27$	$3^{-3} = \frac{1}{27}$

5-1
Rational Exponents and Properties of Exponents

SavvasRealize.com

A. Who is correct, Casey or Jacinta? Explain.

B. Reason What is the most likely error that was made?

HABITS OF MIND

Look for Relationships How do you know when exponential expressions are equivalent? Explain.

Notes

Assess

EXAMPLE 1

Try It! Write Radicals Using Rational Exponents

1. What does $2^{\frac{1}{3}}$ equal? Explain.

EXAMPLE 2

Try It! Use the Product of Powers Property to Solve Equations With Rational Exponents

2. What is the solution of $\left(2^{\frac{x}{4}}\right)\left(2^{\frac{x}{6}}\right) = 2^3$?

EXAMPLE 3

Try It! Use the Power of Power Property to Solve Equations With Rational Exponents

3. What is the solution of each equation?

   a. $256^{x+2} = 4^{3x+9}$

   b. $\left(\frac{1}{8}\right)^{\frac{x}{2}-1} = \left(\frac{1}{4}\right)^{\frac{x}{3}}$

HABITS OF MIND

Communicate Precisely When is the value of an expression undefined? Explain.

EXAMPLE 4

Try It! Use the Power of a Product Property to Solve Equations With Rational Exponents

4. When the side length of Blanket A is multiplied by $2^{\frac{1}{2}}$ the result is 6 yards. Find the area of Blanket A.

EXAMPLE 5

Try It! Use the Quotient of Powers Property to Solve Equations With Rational Exponents

5. What is the value of *x* if the side length of Terrarium A is 3 times greater than the side length of Terrarium B?

HABITS OF MIND

Look for Relationships Can you use the same properties of exponents for expressions with rational exponents as you do when computing with integers? Explain.

Assess

Do You UNDERSTAND?

1. ESSENTIAL QUESTION What are the properties of rational exponents and how are they used to solve problems?

2. **Communicate Precisely** A square has an area of 15 ft^2. What are two ways of expressing its side lengths?

3. **Look for Relationships** If $3^x = 3^y$, what is the relationship between x and y?

4. **Error Analysis** Corey wrote $\sqrt[3]{4^2}$ as $4^{\frac{3}{2}}$. What error did Corey make?

5. **Reason** When is it useful to have rational exponents instead of radicals?

6. **Vocabulary** How are *rational exponents* different than whole number exponents? How are they the same?

Do You KNOW HOW?

Write each radical using rational exponents.

7. $\sqrt{7}$

8. $\sqrt{15}$

9. $\sqrt[3]{6^4}$

10. $\sqrt[3]{2^3}$

11. $\sqrt[4]{2^4}$

12. $\sqrt{8^3}$

Solve each equation.

13. $\left(2^{\frac{x}{3}}\right)\left(2^{\frac{x}{4}}\right) = 2^5$

14. $\left(4^{\frac{x}{2}}\right)\left(4^{\frac{x}{5}}\right) = 4^8$

15. $64^{x+1} = 4^{x+7}$

16. $16^{(x-3)} = 2^{(x-6)}$

17. $\left(\frac{1}{243}\right)^{-\frac{x}{3}} = \left(\frac{1}{9}\right)^{-\frac{x}{2}+1}$

18. $\left(\frac{1}{36}\right)^{(x-4)} = \left(\frac{1}{216}\right)^{x+1}$

Activity

5-2 Exponential Functions

SavvasRealize.com

EXPLORE & REASON

Use two pieces of $8\frac{1}{2}$ by 11 paper. Fold one of the pieces of paper accordion-style for five folds. Fold the other in half for five folds. After each fold, unfold each piece of paper and count the total number of rectangular sections.

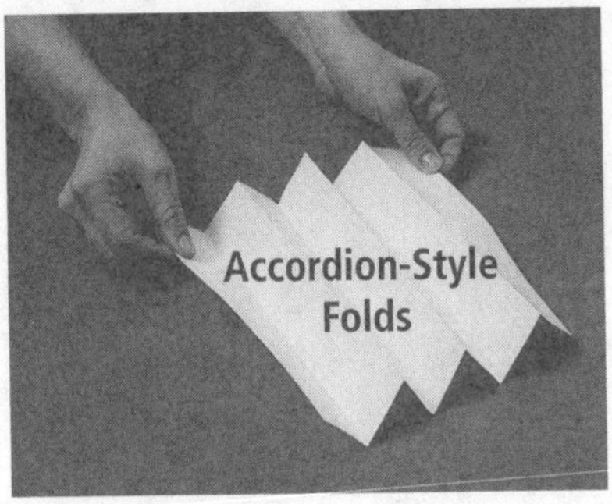

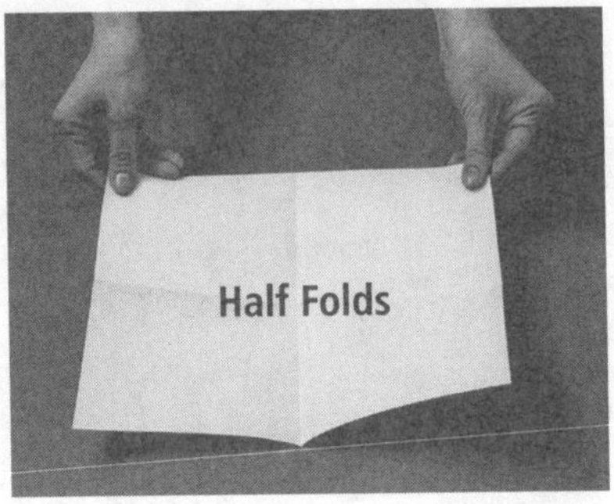

A. Find the pattern relating the number of folds to the number of sections for each folding style. What do you notice?

B. **Make Sense and Persevere** Explain why the two different folded pieces of paper produce different results.

HABITS OF MIND

Model With Mathematics Describe another situation that you could represent using an exponential function.

Notes

Assess

EXAMPLE 1

Try It! Key Features of Exponential Functions

1. Identify the key features of the function $f(x) = b^x$ for $b = 2$ and $b = \frac{1}{2}$ similar.

EXAMPLE 2

Try It! Graph Exponential Functions

2. How long will it take for the virus to spread to 50,000 computers?

HABITS OF MIND

Use Appropriate Tools Suppose the spread of another virus is modeled by the function $g(x) = 5^x$. If it takes the virus five and a half hours to spread, what tools could you use to investigate the function $g(x) = 5^x$?

EXAMPLE 3

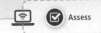

Try It! Write Exponential Functions

3. Write an exponential function for each set of points.

   a. (0, 3), (1, 12), (2, 48), (3, 192), and (4, 768)

   b. (0, 2,187), (1, 729), (2, 243), (3, 81), and (4, 27)

EXAMPLE 4

Try It! Compare Linear and Exponential Functions

4. Identify each function as linear or exponential. Explain.

   a. $f(x)$ equals the number of branches at level x in a tree diagram, where at each level each branch extends into 4 branches.

   b. $f(x)$ equals the number of boxes in row x of a stack in which each row increases by 2 boxes.

HABITS OF MIND

Use Structure In an exponential function, why is a a nonzero constant and $b \neq 1$?

Do You UNDERSTAND?

1. ESSENTIAL QUESTION What are the characteristics of exponential functions?

2. **Look for Relationships** How can you tell whether the graph of a function of form $f(x) = ab^x$, where $a > 0$, will increase or decrease from left to right?

3. **Make Sense and Persevere** Why is $b \neq 1$ a condition for $f(x) = ab^x$?

4. **Error Analysis** Martin says that $f(x) = 2(4)^x$ starts at 4 and has constant ratio of 2. What error did Martin make? Explain.

Do You KNOW HOW?

Graph each function.

5. $f(x) = 3^x$

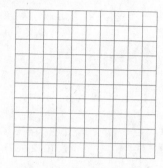

6. $f(x) = \left(\frac{1}{4}\right)^x$

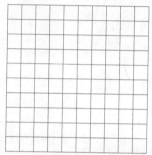

Write each exponential function.

7.

x	$f(x)$
0	4
1	2
2	1
3	$\frac{1}{2}$
4	$\frac{1}{4}$

8.

x	$f(x)$
0	3
1	6
2	12
3	24
4	48

Activity

5-3 Exponential Growth and Decay

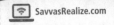

SavvasRealize.com

EXPLORE & REASON

Cindy is buying a new car and wants to learn how the value of her car will change over time. Insurance actuaries predict the future value of cars using depreciation functions. One such function is applied to the car whose declining value is shown.

Years After Purchase	Value
0 yr	\$10,000
1 yr	\$8,520
2 yr	\$7,213
3 yr	\$6,100
4 yr	\$5,210

A. Describe how the value of the car decreases from year to year.

B. **Model With Mathematics** What kind of function would explain this type of pattern?

C. Given your answer to Part B, what is needed to find the function the actuary is using? Explain.

HABITS OF MIND

Make Sense and Persevere What is the constant ratio for the declining values?

Notes

Assess

EXAMPLE 1

Try It! Exponential Growth

1. The population of Valleytown is also 5,000, with an annual increase of 1,000. Can the expected population for Valleytown be modeled with an exponential growth function? Explain.

EXAMPLE 2

Try It! Exponential Models of Growth

2. a. What will be the difference after 15 years if the interest is compounded semiannually rather than quarterly?

   b. What would be the difference in after 15 years if the interest is compounded monthly rather than quarterly?

HABITS OF MIND

Communicate Precisely Explain why the total value increases the more times a value is compounded.

EXAMPLE 3

Try It! Exponential Decay

3. Suppose the number of views decreases by 20% per day. In how many days will the number of views per day be less than 1,000?

Assess

EXAMPLE 4

Try It! Exponential Models of Decay

4. How would the average rate of change over the same intervals be affected if the population increased at a rate of 8%?

EXAMPLE 5

Try It! Exponential Growth and Decay

5. Explain how to use tables on a graphing calculator to answer this question.

HABITS OF MIND

Model With Mathematics What are the key differences in the algebraic representations of exponential growth and decay? Explain.

Do You UNDERSTAND?

1. ESSENTIAL QUESTION What kinds of situations can be modeled with exponential growth or exponential decay?

2. **Vocabulary** What is the difference between simple interest and *compound interest*?

3. **Error Analysis** LaTanya says that the growth factor of $f(x) = 100(1.25)^x$ is 25%. What mistake did LaTanya make? Explain.

4. **Look for Relationships** Why is the growth factor $1 + r$ for an exponential growth function?

Do You KNOW HOW?

Write an exponential growth or decay function for each situation.

5. initial value of 100 increasing at a rate of 5%

6. initial value of 1,250 increasing at a rate of 25%

7. initial value of 512 decreasing at a rate of 50%

8. initial value of 10,000 decreasing at a rate of 12%

9. What is the difference in the value after 10 years of an initial investment of \$2,000 at 5% annual interest when the interest is compounded quarterly rather than annually?

EXPLORE & REASON

A seating plan is being designed for Section 12 of a new stadium.

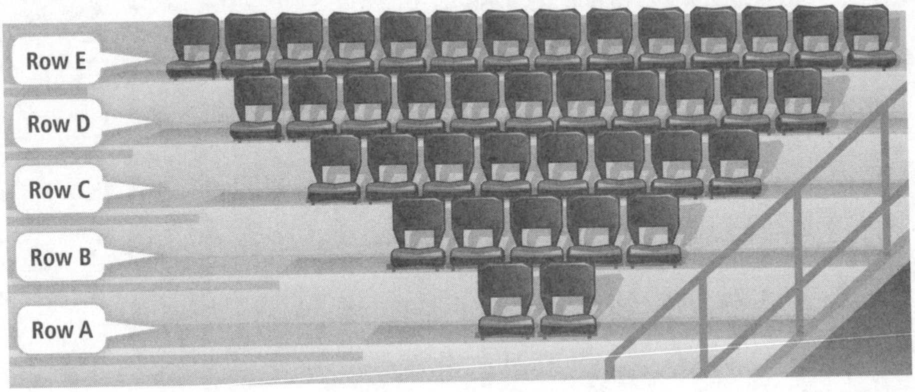

A. Describe the pattern.

B. Write an equation for this pattern.

C. **Use Structure** Row Z of Section 12 must have at least 75 seats. If the pattern continues, does this seating plan meet that requirement? Justify your answer.

HABITS OF MIND

Use Appropriate Tools When is using a diagram the best tool to determine the number of seats in a given row? Explain.

Assess

EXAMPLE 1

Try It! Identify Arithmetic and Geometric Sequences

1. Is each sequence an arithmetic or a geometric sequence? Explain.
   a. 1, 2.2, 4.84, 10.648, 23.4256, ...
   b. 1, 75, 149, 223, 297, ...

EXAMPLE 2

Try It! Write the Recursive Formula For a Sequence

2. Write the recursive formulas for the geometric sequence 3,072, 768, 192, 48, 12, ...

HABITS OF MIND

Make Sense and Persevere Explain why a common ratio in a geometric sequence cannot be zero.

EXAMPLE 3

Try It! Use the Explicit Formula

3. What is the 12th term of the sequence described?
   Initial condition is 3
   recursive formula is $a_n = 6(a_{n-1})$

EXAMPLE 4

Try It! Connect Geometric Sequences and Exponential Functions

4. How many subscribers will there be in Week 9 if the initial number of subscribers is 10?

EXAMPLE 5

Try It! Apply the Recursive and Explicit Formulas

5. The formula $a_n = 1.5(a_{n-1})$ with an initial value of 40 describes a sequence. Use the explicit formula to determine the 5th term of the sequence.

HABITS OF MIND

Reason What is the relationship between the explicit formula and the recursive formula? Explain.

Do You UNDERSTAND?

1. ESSENTIAL QUESTION How are geometric sequences related to exponential functions?

2. **Vocabulary** How are *geometric sequences* similar to arithmetic sequences? How are they different?

3. **Error Analysis** For a geometric sequence with $a_1 = 3$ and a common ratio r of 1.25, Jamie writes $a_n = 1.25 \cdot (3)^{n-1}$. What mistake did Jamie make?

4. **Generalize** Is a sequence geometric if each term in the sequence is x times greater than the preceding term?

Do You KNOW HOW?

Determine whether the sequence is an arithmetic or a geometric sequence. If it is geometric, what is the common ratio?

5. 30, 6, 1.2, 0.24, 0.048, ...

6. 0.5, 2, 8, 32, 148, ...

Write the recursive formula for each geometric sequence.

7. 640, 160, 40, 10, 2.5, ...

8. 2, 5, 12.5, 31.25, 78.125, ...

9. What is the recursive formula for a sequence with the following explicit formula?
$a_n = 1.25 \cdot (3)^{n-1}$

10. A sequence has an initial value of 25 and a common ratio of 1.8. How can you write the sequence as a function?

Activity

5-5
Transformations of Exponential Functions

SavvasRealize.com

MODEL & DISCUSS

A radio station uses the function $f(x) = 100(3)^x$ to model the growth of Band A's fan base.

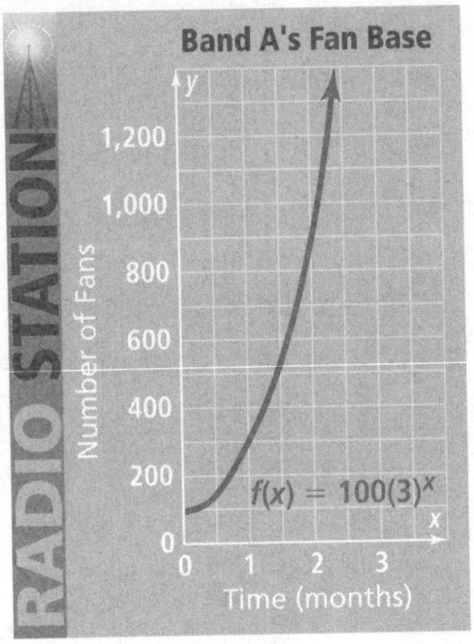

A. What would the graph of the function look like for Band B with a fan base growing twice as fast as Band A's fan base?

B. Compare and contrast the two graphs.

C. Look for Relationships Suppose Band C starts with a fan base of 200 fans that is growing twice as fast as Band A's fan base. Compare and contrast this new function with the previous two functions.

HABITS OF MIND

Look for Relationships Is it possible for the graph of a function to have a negative value for x? Explain.

Notes

Assess

EXAMPLE 1

Try It! Vertical Translations of Graphs of Exponential Functions

1. a. How does the graph of $g(x) = 2^x + 1$ compare to the graph of $f(x) = 2^x$?

   b. How does the graph of $j(x) = 2^x - 1$ compare to the graph of $f(x) = 2^x$?

EXAMPLE 2

Try It! Horizontal Translations of Graphs of Exponential Functions

2. Compare the graph of each function with the graph of $f(x) = 2^x$. What effect does h have on the graph of each?

   a. $g(x) = 2^{x+2}$

   b. $j(x) = 2^{x-2}$

HABITS OF MIND

Use Structure Describe how the function that results in a vertical translation is different from a function that results in a horizontal translation.

Assess

EXAMPLE 3

Try It! Compare Two Different Transformations of $f(x) = 2^x$

3. a. The graph of the function b is a vertical translation of the graph of $a(x) = 3^x$, and has a y-intercept of 0. How does the graph of $c(x) = 3^x + 1$ compare to the graph of b?

b. How does the graph of $m(x) = 3^x - 3$ compare to the graph of $p(x) = 3^x + 4$?

HABITS OF MIND

Communicate Precisely What effect does inserting a different constant into an exponential function have on the transformation of a function? Explain.

Assess

Do You UNDERSTAND?

1. ESSENTIAL QUESTION How do changes in an exponential function relate to translations of its graph?

2. **Communicate Precisely** How is the effect of k on the graph of $a^x + k$ similar to the effect of h on the graph of a^{x-h}? How is it different?

3. **Error Analysis** Tariq graphs $g(x) = 2^x + 6$ by translating the graph of $f(x) = 2^x$ six units right. What mistake did Tariq make?

4. **Reason** As the value of k switches from a positive to a negative number, what is the effect on the graph of $f(x) = 2^{x+k}$?

5. **Use Structure** The general form of vertical translations of exponential functions is $f(x) = a^x + k$. The general form of horizontal translations of exponential functions is $f(x) = a^{x-h}$. Why do you think one involves addition and one involves subtraction?

Do You KNOW HOW?

Compare the graph of each function to the graph of $f(x) = 2^x$.

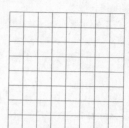

6. $g(x) = 2^x + 1$

7. $p(x) = 2^{x-1}$

8. $j(x) = 2^x - 4$

9. $g(x) = 2^{x+1}$

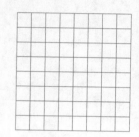

10. Compare the function represented by the graph of $g(x) = 2^x - 3$ to the function represented by the table.

x	$h(x)$
−2	1.25
−1	1.5
0	2
1	3
2	5

Compare the graph of each function to the graph of $f(x) = 0.4^x$.

11. $g(x) = 0.4^{x+1}$

12. $p(x) = 0.4^{x-1}$

13. $j(x) = 0.4^x + 1$

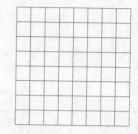

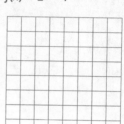

14. $g(x) = 0.4^x - 1$

Video

Big Time Pay Back

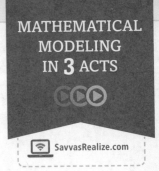

MATHEMATICAL MODELING IN 3 ACTS

SavvasRealize.com

Most people agree that investing your money is a good idea. Some people might advise you to put money into a bank savings account. Other people might say that you should invest in the stock market. Still others think that buying bonds is the best investment option.

Is a bank savings account a good way to let your money grow? Just how much money can you make from a savings account? In the Mathematical Modeling in 3 Acts lesson, you'll see an intriguing situation about an investment option.

ACT 1 Identify the Problem

1. What is the first question that comes to mind after watching the video?

2. Write down the main question you will answer about what you saw in the video.

3. Make an initial conjecture that answers this main question.

4. Explain how you arrived at your conjecture.

5. Write a number that you know is too small.

6. Write a number that you know is too large.

7. What information will be useful to know to answer the main question? How can you get it? How will you use that information?

ACT 2 Develop a Model

8. Use the math that you have learned in this topic to refine your conjecture.

ACT 3 Interpret the Results

9. Is your refined conjecture between the highs and lows you set up earlier?

10. Did your refined conjecture match the actual answer exactly? If not, what might explain the difference?

6-1 Measuring Segments and Angles

EXPLORE & REASON

A teacher labels two points on the number line.

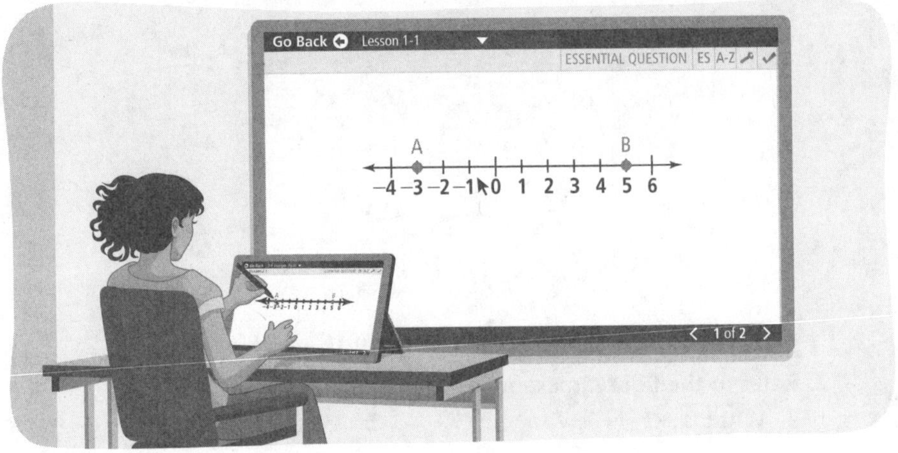

A. What are some methods for finding the distance between points *A* and *B*?

B. Construct Arguments Which method of finding the distance is the best? Explain.

HABITS OF MIND

Generalize Which strategy could you apply to find the distance between any two numbers on the number line?

EXAMPLE 1

Try It! Find Segment Lengths

1. Refer to the figure in Example 1. How can you find the length of $\overline{AC}$?

EXAMPLE 2

Try It! Find the Length of a Segment

2. Refer to the figure in Example 2.

   a. What is JK?

   b. What is KM?

EXAMPLE 3

Try It! Use the Segment Addition Postulate

3. Points J, K, and L are collinear.

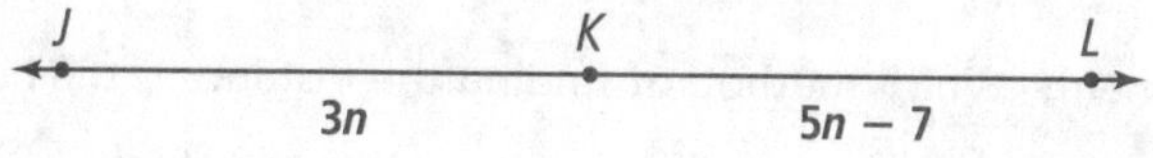

   a. If $JL = 25$, what is n?

   b. What is JK? KL?

HABITS OF MIND

Construct Arguments Gina says that for any segment $\overline{AB}$ on a number line, $AB = BA$. Do you agree? Explain.

EXAMPLE 4

Try It! Use the Protractor Postulate to Measure an Angle

4. Refer to the figure in Example 4.
   a. What is $m\angle AEC$?
   b. What is $m\angle BED$?

EXAMPLE 5

Try It! Use the Angle Addition Postulate to Solve Problems

5. Refer to Example 5. Can the lighting designer use a spotlight with a 33° beam angle that can rotate 25° to the left and right to light all of the objects on the stage?

EXAMPLE 6

Try It! Use Congruent Angles and Congruent Segments

6. a. If $m\angle NOP = 31$ and $m\angle NOQ = 114$, what is $m\angle ROQ$?

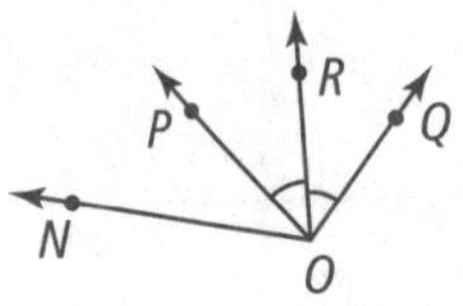

   b. In the figure in Part B above, suppose $CD = 11.5$ cm, $DE = 5.3$ cm, and the perimeter of the figure is 73.8 cm. What is GE?

HABITS OF MIND

Use Appropriate Tools If M is in the interior of $\angle ABC$, would be helpful to use a diagram to compare $m\angle ABM = m\angle ABC$? Explain.

Do You UNDERSTAND?

1. **ESSENTIAL QUESTION** How are the properties of segments and angles used to determine their measures?

2. **Error Analysis** Ella wrote $AB = |-1 + 5| = 4$. Explain Ella's error.

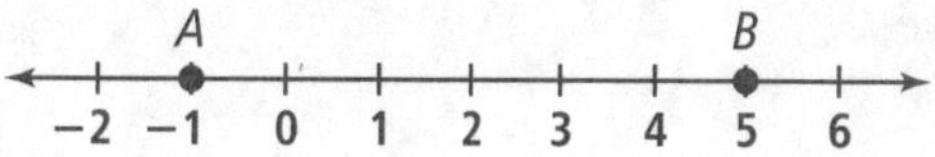

3. **Vocabulary** What does it mean for segments to be congruent? What does it mean for angles to be congruent?

4. **Make Sense and Persevere** Suppose M is a point in the interior of $\angle JKL$. If $m\angle MKL = 42$ and $m\angle JKL = 84$, what is $m\angle JKM$?

Do You KNOW HOW?

Find the length of each segment.

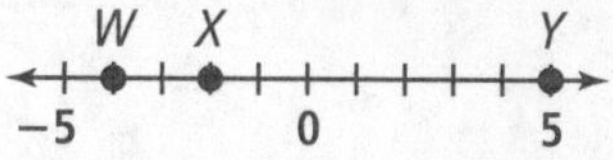

5. $\overline{WX}$

6. $\overline{WY}$

7. Points A, B, and C are collinear and B is between A and C. Given $AB = 12$ and $AC = 19$, what is BC?

8. Given $m\angle JML = 80$ and $m\angle KML = 33$, what is $m\angle JMK$?

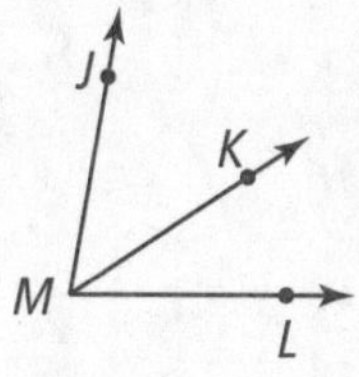

Activity

6-2 Basic Constructions

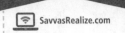

SavvasRealize.com

EXPLORE & REASON

Using a compass, make a design using only circles like the one shown.

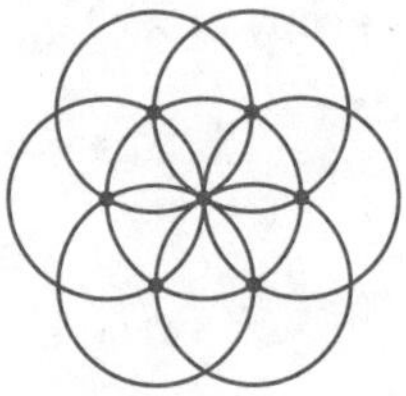

A. What instructions can you give to another student so they can make a copy of your design?

B. **Make Sense and Persevere** Use a ruler to draw straight line segments to connect points where the circles intersect. Are any of the segments that you drew the same length? If so, why do you think they are?

HABITS OF MIND

Communicate Precisely What mathematical terms or concepts can you use to describe your design?

Notes

Assess

EXAMPLE 1

Try It! Copy a Segment

1. How can you construct a copy of $\overline{XY}$?

EXAMPLE 2

Try It! Copy an Angle

2. How can you construct a copy of $\angle B$?

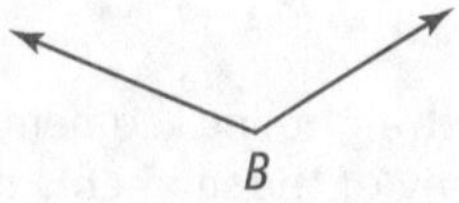

HABITS OF MIND

Construct Arguments Leo says a copy of a segment or angle is always congruent to the original, even if the orientation of the copy is different from the orientation of the original. Construct an argument to support or refute Leo's statement.

EXAMPLE 3

Try It! Construct a Perpendicular Bisector

3. How can you construct the perpendicular bisector of $\overline{JK}$?

EXAMPLE 4

Try It! Construct an Angle Bisector

4. How can you construct the angle bisector of $\angle G$?

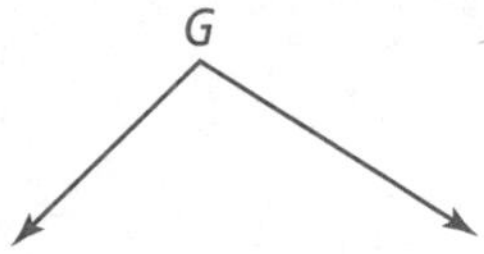

EXAMPLE 5

Try It! Use Constructions

5. Where should the sculpture be placed if it is to be center-aligned with the museum entrance and the center of the ticket sales desk?

HABITS OF MIND

Look for Relationships How is constructing a perpendicular bisector similar to constructing an angle bisector?

Do You UNDERSTAND?

1. **ESSENTIAL QUESTION** How are a straightedge and compass used to make basic constructions?

2. **Error Analysis** Chris tries to copy $\angle T$ but is unable to make an exact copy. Explain Chris's error.

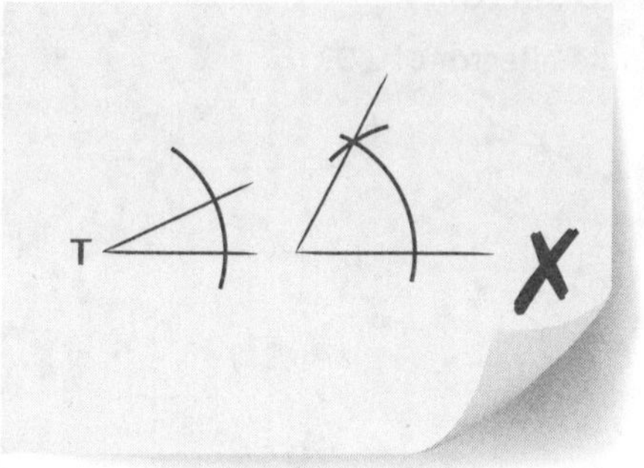

3. **Vocabulary** What is the difference between a line that is perpendicular to a segment and the perpendicular bisector of a segment?

4. **Look for Relationships** Darren is copying $\triangle ABC$. First, he constructs $\overline{DE}$ as a copy of $\overline{AB}$. Next, he constructs $\angle D$ as a copy of $\angle A$, using $\overline{DE}$ as one of the sides. Explain what he needs to do to complete the copy of the triangle.

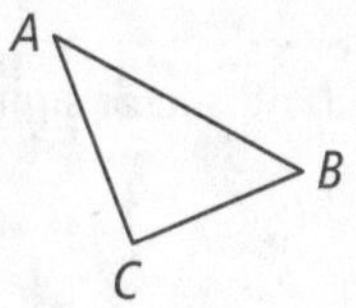

Do You KNOW HOW?

Construct a copy of each segment, and then construct its perpendicular bisector.

5.

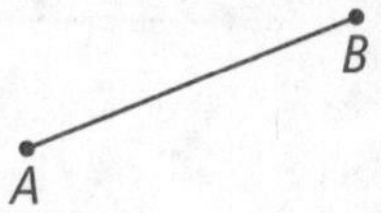

6.

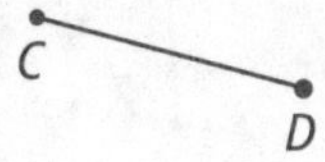

Construct a copy of each angle, and then construct its bisector.

7.

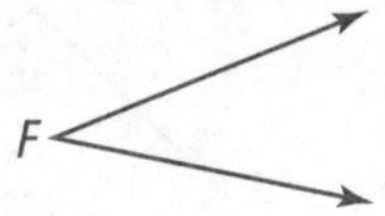

8.

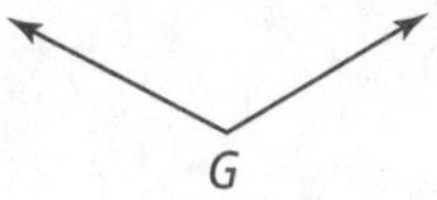

9. A new sidewalk is perpendicular to and bisecting the existing sidewalk. At the point where new sidewalk meets the fence around the farmer's market, a gate is needed. At about what point should the gate be placed?

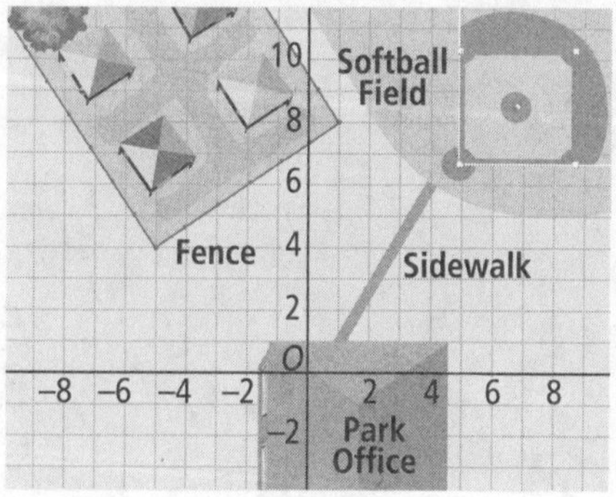

Activity

6-3 Midpoint and Distance

SavvasRealize.com

MODEL & SOLVE

LaTanya is decorating her living room and draws a floor plan to help look at placement.

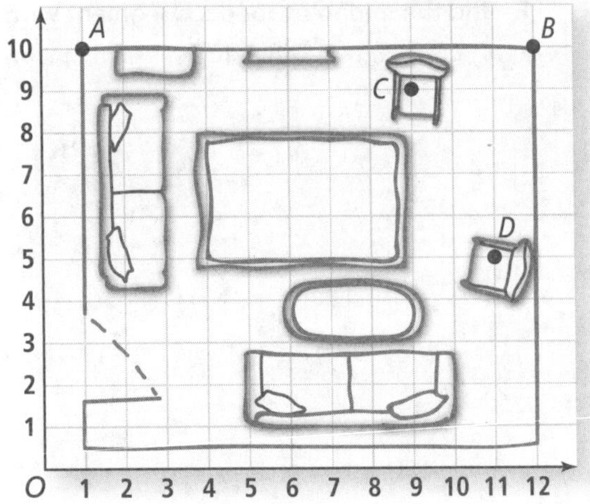

A. LaTanya wants to hang a picture at the center of the back wall. How do you find the point at the center between A and B?

B. Communicate Precisely LaTanya wants to place a lamp halfway between the chairs at points C and D. How can you find the point where the lamp should go?

HABITS OF MIND

Use Appropriate Tools What tools did you use to help you answer the questions? Why was it helpful to use the tools you did?

Notes

Assess

EXAMPLE 1

Try It! Find a Midpoint

1. Find the midpoint for each segment with the given endpoints.

   a. $C(-2, 5)$ and $D(8, -12)$

   b. $E(2.5, -7)$ and $F(-6.2, -3.8)$

EXAMPLE 2

Try It! Partition a Segment

2. Find the coordinates of each point described.

   a. $\frac{7}{10}$ of the way from A to B.

   b. $\frac{4}{5}$ of the way from B to A.

HABITS OF MIND

Generalize Is there a mathematical rule for finding the coordinates of the point R that is fraction q of the way from point $P(x_1, y_1)$ to $Q(x_2, y_2)$? Explain.

Notes

Assess

EXAMPLE 3

Try It! Derive the Distance Formula

3. Tavon claims that $d = \sqrt{(x_1 - x_2)^2 + (y_1 - y_2)^2}$ can also be used to find distance between two points. Is he correct? Explain.

EXAMPLE 4

Try It! Find the Distance

4. How far does the shortstop need to throw the ball to reach the first baseman? Round to the nearest tenth of a foot.

HABITS OF MIND

Look for Relationships How do you relate the distance formula between two points to the Pythagorean Theorem?

Do You UNDERSTAND?

1. **ESSENTIAL QUESTION** How are the midpoint and length of a segment on the coordinate plane determined?

2. **Error Analysis** Corey calculated the midpoint of $\overline{AB}$ with $A(-3, 5)$ and $B(1, 7)$. What is Corey's error?

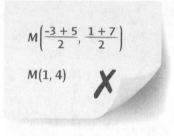

$$M\left(\frac{-3+5}{2}, \frac{1+7}{2}\right)$$

$M(1, 4)$ ✗

3. **Vocabulary** If M is the midpoint of $\overline{PQ}$, what is the relationship between PM and MQ? Between PM and PQ?

4. **Reason** Is it possible for $\overline{PQ}$ to have two distinct midpoints, $M_1(a, b)$ and $M_2(c, d)$? Explain.

Do You KNOW HOW?

$\overline{PQ}$ has endpoints at $P(-5, 4)$ and $Q(7, -5)$.

5. What is the midpoint of $\overline{PQ}$?

6. What are the coordinates of the point $\frac{2}{3}$ of the way from P to Q?

7. What is the length of $\overline{PQ}$?

8. A chair lift at a ski resort travels along the cable as shown.

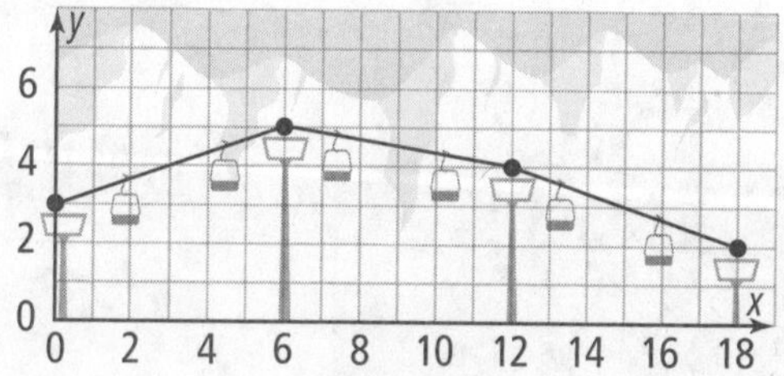

1 unit = 10 ft

How long is the cable? Round your answer to the nearest whole foot.

Activity

6-4 Inductive Reasoning

SavvasRealize.com

EXPLORE & REASON

When points on a circle are connected, the line segments divide the circle into a number of regions, as shown.

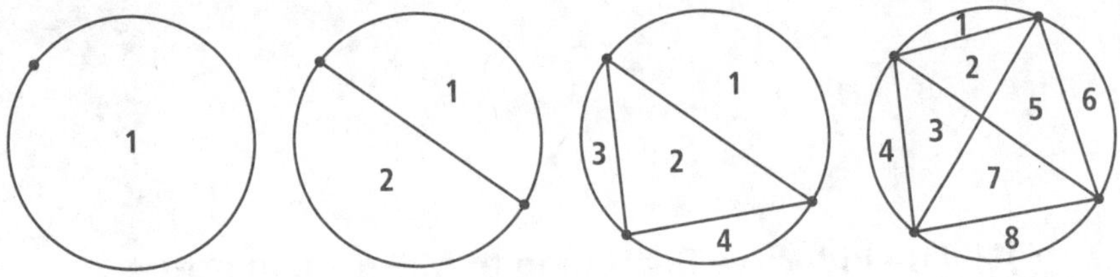

A. How does the number of regions change when another point is added?

B. Look for Relationships Using the pattern you observed, make a prediction about the number of regions formed by connecting 5 points on a circle. Make a drawing to test your prediction. Is your prediction correct?

HABITS OF MIND

Generalize Does an observation of a pattern always prove a relationship? Explain.

Notes

Assess

EXAMPLE 1

Try It! Use Inductive Reasoning to Extend a Pattern

1. What appear to be the next two terms in each sequence?

   a. 800, 400, 200, 100,...

   b. 18, 24, 32, $\frac{128}{3}$,...

EXAMPLE 2

Try It! Use Inductive Reasoning to Make a Conjecture

2. a. How many dots are in the 5th and 6th terms of the pattern?

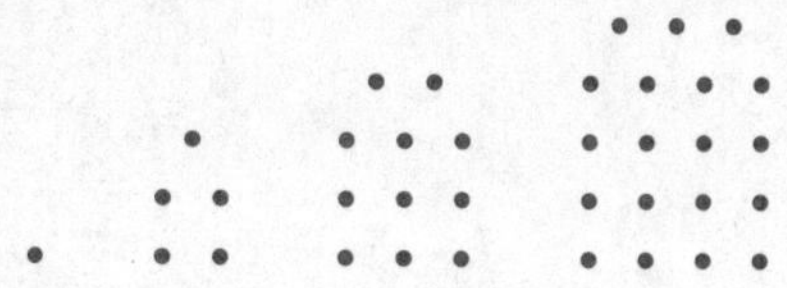

   b. What conjecture can you make about the number of dots in the *n*th term of the pattern?

EXAMPLE 3

Try It! Use a Conjecture to Make a Prediction

3. Based on the data, about how many members would you expect the chess club to have in its 5th year?

Year	1	2	3	4
Club Members	10	13	17	22

HABITS OF MIND

Look for Relationships What strategies can you use to find patterns in numbers presented in a sequence or in a table? What strategies can you use to find patterns with dots or other visual patterns?

EXAMPLE 4

Try It! Find a Counterexample to Show a Conjecture is False

4. What is a counterexample that shows the statement, *the sum of two composite numbers must be a composite number,* is false?

EXAMPLE 5

Try It! Test a Conjecture

5. For each conjecture, test the conjecture with several more examples or find a counterexample to disprove it.
   a. For every integer n, the value of n^2 is positive.

   b. A number is divisible by 4 if the last two digits are divisible by 4.

HABITS OF MIND

Construct Arguments Tyler says that only one example is needed to prove that a conjecture is true. Do you agree?

Assess

Do You UNDERSTAND?

1. ESSENTIAL QUESTION How is inductive reasoning used to recognize mathematical relationships?

2. **Error Analysis** Esteban made the following drawing and then stated this conjecture: "The altitude of a triangle always lies inside of or along the side of the triangle." What error did Esteban make?

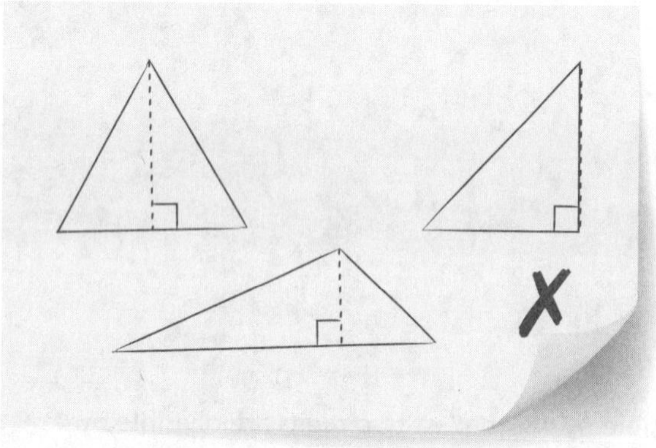

3. **Vocabulary** What type of statement results from inductive reasoning?

Do You KNOW HOW?

4. What appear to be the next three numbers in the pattern?

   4, 11, 18, 25,...

5. What conjecture can you make about the number of regions created by n unique diameters?

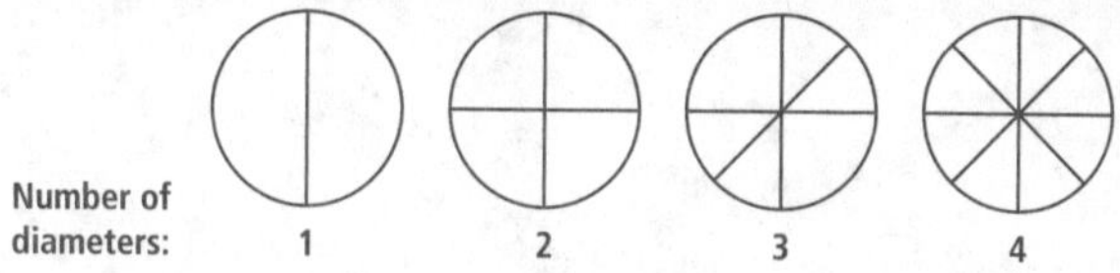

6. Can you find four examples that are true or a counterexample for the following statement?

   For every integer n, the value of $n^2 + 1$ is odd.

Video

MATHEMATICAL MODELING IN 3 ACTS

SavvasRealize.com

The Mystery Spokes

Some photos are taken in such a way that it is difficult to determine exactly what the picture shows. Sometimes it's because the photo is a close up part of an object, and you do not see the entire object. Other times, it might be because the photographer used special effects when taking the photo.

You can often use clues from the photo to determine what is in the photo and also what the rest of the object might look like. What clues would you look for? Think about this during the Mathematical Modeling in 3 Acts lesson.

ACT 1 Identify the Problem

1. What is the first question that comes to mind after watching the video?

2. Write down the Main Question you will answer.

3. Make an initial conjecture that answers this Main Question.

4. Explain how you arrived at your conjecture.

5. Write a number that you know is too small.

6. Write a number that you know is too large.

ACT 2 Develop a Model

7. Use the math that you have learned in the topic to refine your conjecture.

ACT 3 Interpret the Results

8. Is your refined conjecture between the highs and lows you set up earlier?

9. Did your refined conjecture match the actual answer exactly? If not, what might explain the difference?

Activity

6-5 Conditional Statements

SavvasRealize.com

EXPLORE & REASON

If-then statements show a cause and effect. The table shows some if-then statements.

Cause	Effect
If it is raining	then it is spring.
If x and y are whole numbers	then their difference, $x - y$, is a whole number.
If water is heated	then it boils.
If a triangle has a right angle	then it is a right triangle.
If your favorite color is blue	then you are a good speller.

A. Construct Arguments Determine whether each effect is always true for the given cause, or is not necessarily true for the given cause. For the effects that are not necessarily true, how could you change them to make them always true?

B. Write some if-then statements of your own. Write two statements that are always true and two statements that are not necessarily true.

HABITS OF MIND

Look for Relationships You have used the word *hypothesis* and *conclusion* in other classes. How are their meanings the same as or different from the definitions in geometry?

Notes

Assess

EXAMPLE 1

Try It! Write a Conditional Statement

1. Write each statement as a conditional.

   a. A triangle with all angles congruent is equilateral.

   b. Alberto can go to the movies if he washes the car.

EXAMPLE 2

Try It! Find a Truth Value of a Conditional

2. What is the truth value of each conditional? Explain your reasoning.

   a. If a quadrilateral has a right angle, then it is a rectangle.

   b. If X is the midpoint of $\overline{AB}$, then X lies on $\overline{AB}$.

EXAMPLE 3

Try It! Write and Determine the Truth Value of a Converse

3. Write and determine the truth value of the converse of the conditional.

   a. If a polygon is a quadrilateral, then it has four sides.

   b. If two angles are complementary, then their angle measures add to 90.

Assess

EXAMPLE 4

Try It! Write and Evaluate the Truth Value of an Inverse and a Contrapositive

4. Write the converse, the inverse, and the contrapositive. What is the truth value of each?

   If today is a weekend day, then tomorrow is Monday.

HABITS OF MIND

Reason What is the truth value of the conditional, "If 11 is an even number, then there are 23 hours in a day?" What are the truth values of the hypothesis and conclusion? Is this true of all conditionals where the hypothesis can never be true?

EXAMPLE 5

Try It! Write and Evaluate a Biconditional

5. Write a biconditional for the following conditional. What is its truth value?

   If two lines intersect at right angles, then they are perpendicular.

EXAMPLE 6

Try It! Identify the Conditionals in a Biconditional

6. What are the two conditionals implied by the biconditional?

   The product of two numbers is negative if and only if the numbers have opposite signs.

HABITS OF MIND

Generalize How is a biconditional similar to giving a definition? Can you think of a definition in geometry and express it as a biconditional?

Do You UNDERSTAND?

1. ESSENTIAL QUESTION How do if-then statements describe mathematical relationships.

2. **Error Analysis** Allie was asked to write the inverse of the following conditional.

   If it is sunny, then I use sunscreen.

   What error did Allie make?

If it is not sunny, then
I use sunscreen.
X

3. **Vocabulary** Which term is used to describe the opposite of a statement?

4. **Generalize** How do you write the converse of a conditional? How do you write the contrapositive of a conditional?

5. **Communicate Precisely** Explain how the inverse and the contrapositive of a conditional are alike and how they are different.

Do You KNOW HOW?

6. Write the following statement as a biconditional.

   A prime number has only 1 and itself as factors.

For Exercises 7–9, use the following conditional.

If a rectangle has an area of 12 m^2, then it has sides of length 3 m and 4 m.

7. What is the hypothesis? What is the conclusion?

8. Assume the hypothesis is false. What is the truth value of the conditional? Assume the hypothesis is true. What would be a counterexample?

9. What are the converse, the inverse, and the contrapositive? What are their truth values?

10. What two conditionals are implied by the following biconditional?

"The city can build new roads if and only if the sales tax is raised to 10%."

Activity

6-6 Deductive Reasoning

SavvasRealize.com

CRITIQUE & EXPLAIN

A deck of 60 game cards are numbered from 1 to 15 on one of four different shapes (triangle, circle, square, and pentagon). A teacher selects five cards and displays four of the cards.

She tells her class that all of the cards she selected have the same shape and asks them to draw a conclusion about the fifth card.

Chen

The fifth card is 11.

Carolina

The fifth card has a circle.

A. Describe how each student might have reached his or her conclusion. Is each student's conclusion valid? Explain.

B. **Make Sense and Persevere** What are other possibilities of the fifth card? What could the teacher say to narrow the possibilities?

HABITS OF MIND

Making Sense and Persevere How else might you represent the situation?

Notes

Assess

EXAMPLE 1 **Try It!** **Determine Whether a Statement Is True**

1. Given that a conditional and its hypothesis are true, can you determine whether the conclusion is true?

EXAMPLE 2 **Try It!** **Apply the Law of Detachment to Draw Real-World and Mathematical Conclusions**

2. Assume that each set of given information is true.

   a. If two angles are congruent, then the measures of the two angles are equal to each other. Angle 1 is congruent to ∠2. What can you logically conclude about the measures of ∠1 and ∠2?

   b. If you finish the race in under 30 minutes, then you win a prize. You finished the race in 26 minutes. What can you logically conclude?

HABITS OF MIND

Generalize In part (a), what would happen if ∠1 was not congruent to ∠2?

Assess

EXAMPLE 3

Try It! Apply the Law of Syllogism to Draw Real-World and Mathematical Conclusions

3. Assume that each set of conditionals is true. Use the Law of Syllogism to draw a conclusion.

   a. If an integer is divisible by 6, it is divisible by 2. If an integer is divisible by 2, then it is an even number.

   b. If it is a holiday, then you don't have to go to school. If it is Labor Day, then it is a holiday.

EXAMPLE 4

Try It! Apply the Laws of Detachment and Syllogism to Draw Conclusions

4. Martin walks his dog before dinner every day. Martin is now eating his dinner. Using the Law of Detachment and the Law of Syllogism, what conclusions can you draw from these true statements?

HABITS OF MIND

Construct Arguments Compare the situations in Examples 3 and 4. What is the same about them? What is different?

Do You UNDERSTAND?

1. **ESSENTIAL QUESTION** How is deductive reasoning different from inductive reasoning?

2. **Error Analysis** Dakota writes the following as an example of using the Law of Detachment. What is her error?

> If my favorite team wins more than 55 games, they win the championship. My team won the championship, so they won more than 55 games.

3. **Vocabulary** What are the differences between the Law of Detachment and the Law of Syllogism?

4. **Use Structure** How can representing sentences and phrases with symbols help you determine whether to apply the Law of Detachment or the Law of Syllogism?

Do You KNOW HOW?

Assume that each set of given information is true.

5. If you have a temperature above 100.4°F, then you have a fever. Casey has a temperature of 101.2°F. What can you conclude about Casey? What rule of inference did you use?

6. If points *A*, *B*, and *C* are collinear with *B* between *A* and *C*, then $AB + BC = AC$. Use the information in the figure shown. What can you conclude about *AC*?

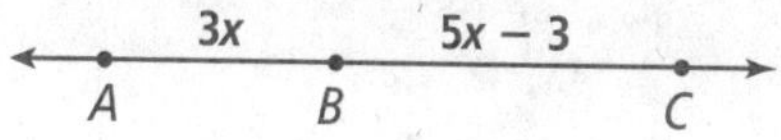

Assume that each set of conditionals is true. Use the Law of Syllogism to write a true conditional.

7. If you eat too much, you get a stomach ache. If you get a stomach ache, you want to rest.

8. If two numbers are odd, the sum of the numbers is even. If a number is even, then the number is divisible by 2.

Activity

6-7 Writing Proofs

SavvasRealize.com

CRITIQUE & EXPLAIN

William solved an equation for x and wrote justifications for each step of his solutions.

$6(14 + x) = 108$	Given
$84 + 6x = 108$	Distributive Property
$6x = 108 - 84$	Subtraction Property of Equality
$6x = 24$	Simplify
$x = 4$	Multiplication Property of Equality

A. **Make Sense and Persevere** Are William's justifications valid at each step? If not, what might you change? Explain.

B. Can you justify another series of steps that result in the same solution for x?

HABITS OF MIND

Use Structure What ideas have you learned before that were useful in evaluating William's solution?

Assess

EXAMPLE 1

Try It! Write a Two-Column Proof

1. Write a two-column proof.

Given: $\overrightarrow{BD}$ bisects $\angle CBE$.

Prove: $\angle ABD \cong \angle FBD$

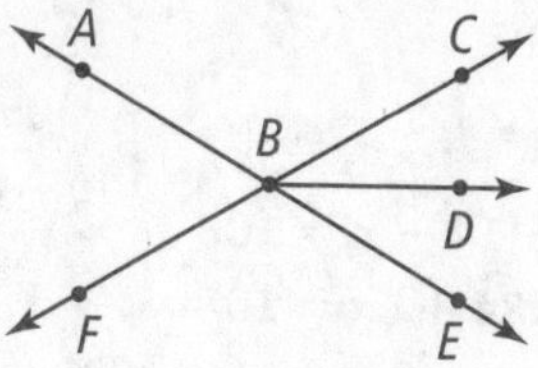

HABITS OF MIND

Use Appropriate Tools What do you know that is not stated in the problem?

EXAMPLE 2

Try It! Apply the Vertical Angles Theorem

2. Find the value of x and the measure of each labeled angle.

a.

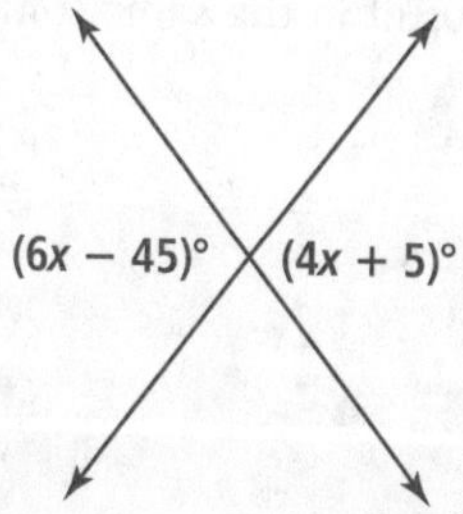

b.

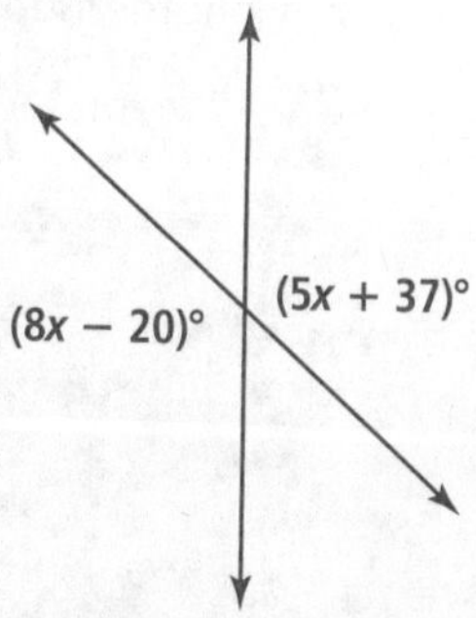

HABITS OF MIND

Communicate Precisely What steps can you take to verify that each solution is correct?

Notes

Assess

EXAMPLE 3

Try It! Write a Paragraph Proof

3. Write a paragraph proof of the Congruent Complements Theorem.

Given: $\angle 1$ and $\angle 2$ are complementary.
$\angle 2$ and $\angle 3$ are complementary.

Prove: $\angle 1 \cong \angle 3$

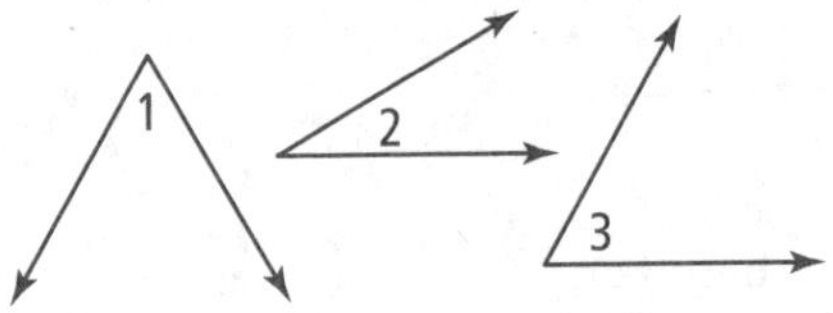

EXAMPLE 4

Try It! Write a Proof Using a Theorem

4. Write a two-column proof.

Given: $m\angle 4 = 35$, $m\angle 1 = m\angle 2 + m\angle 4$

Prove: $m\angle 3 = 70$

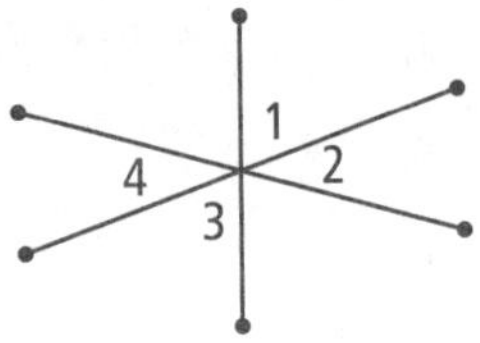

HABITS OF MIND

Reason What properties, theorems, or definitions did you use to prove $m\angle 3 = 70$?

Do You UNDERSTAND?

1. **ESSENTIAL QUESTION** How is deductive reasoning used to prove a theorem?

2. **Error Analysis** Jayden states that based on the Congruent Supplements Theorem, if $m\angle 1 + m\angle 2 = 90$ and if $m\angle 1 + m\angle 3 = 90$, then $\angle 2 \cong \angle 3$. What is the error in Jayden's reasoning?

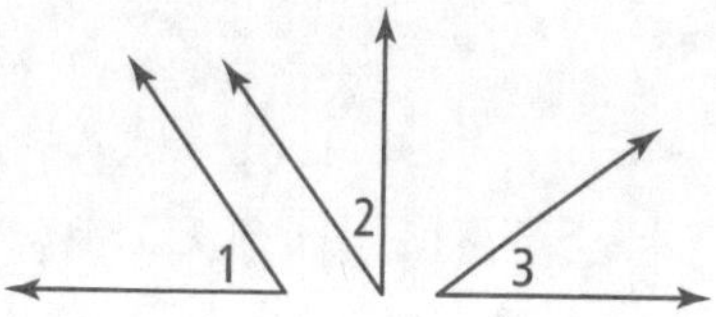

3. **Vocabulary** How is a theorem different from a postulate? How is a theorem different from a conjecture?

4. **Reason** If $\angle 2$ and $\angle 3$ are complementary, how could you use the Vertical Angles Theorem to find $m\angle 1$?

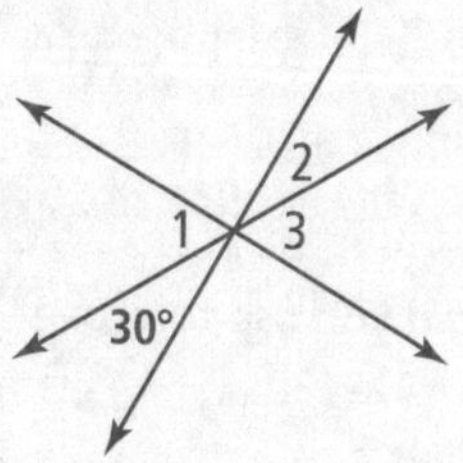

Do You KNOW HOW?

Use the figures to answer Exercises 5–7.

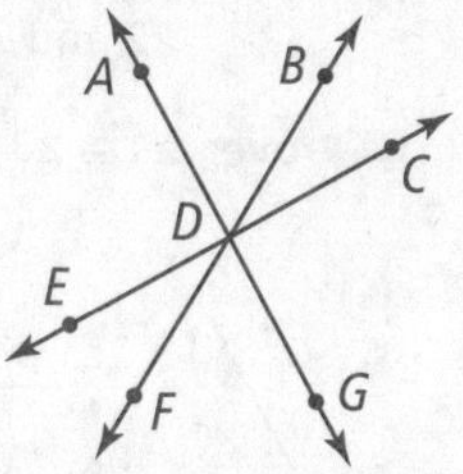

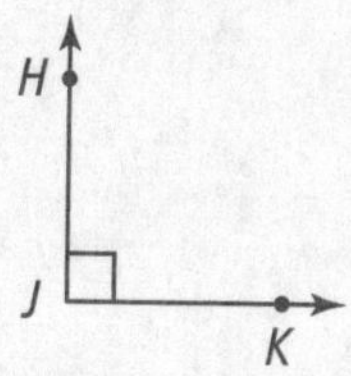

5. What statement could you write in a proof for $m\angle ADC$ using the Angle Addition Postulate as a reason?

6. Could you use the Vertical Angles Theorem as a reason in a proof to state $m\angle ADC = m\angle EDG$ or to state $\angle ADC \cong \angle EDG$? Explain.

7. Given $m\angle ADC = 90$, what reason could you give in a proof to state $\angle ADC \cong \angle HJK$?

8. Leaning Tower of Pisa leans at an angle of about 4° from the vertical, as shown. What equation for the measure of x, the angle it makes from the horizontal, could you use in a proof?

Activity

6-8 Indirect Proof

SavvasRealize.com

CRITIQUE & EXPLAIN

Philip presents the following number puzzle to his friends.

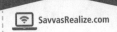

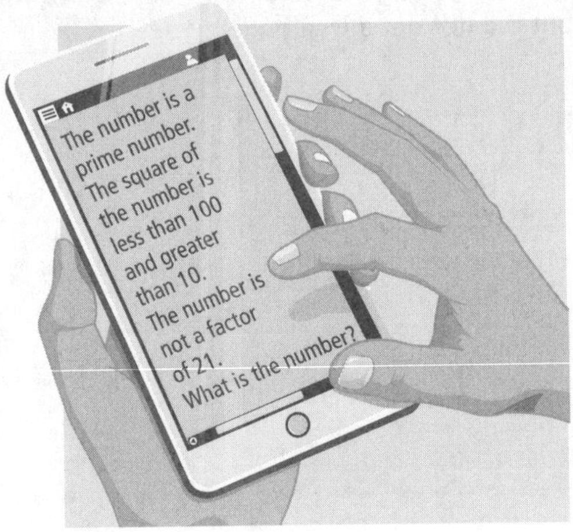
The number is a prime number.
The square of the number is less than 100 and greater than 10.
The number is not a factor of 21.
What is the number?

A. Make Sense and Persevere Philip states that the number must be 7. Explain why this cannot be true.

B. Write your own number puzzle that has an answer of 5. Your friend says the answer is not 5. How do you use the statements of your puzzle to identify the contradiction?

HABITS OF MIND

Communicate Precisely For Part B, explain how you might show that your solution is the answer to the number puzzle.

Notes

Assess

EXAMPLE 1

Try It! Use Indirect Reasoning

1. Use indirect reasoning to draw a conclusion in the following situation.

   A bagel shop gives customers a free bagel on their birthday. Thato went to the bagel shop today but did not get a free bagel.

EXAMPLE 2

Try It! Write an Indirect Proof by Contradiction

2. Write an indirect proof for each statement using proof by contradiction.

   a. If today is a weekend day, then it is Saturday or Sunday.

   b. If you draw an angle that is greater than 90°, it must be obtuse.

Notes

Assess

EXAMPLE 3

Try It! Write an Indirect Proof by Contrapositive

3. Write an indirect proof of each statement using proof by contrapositive.

a. If today is Wednesday, then tomorrow is Thursday.

b. If a whole number is between 1 and 4, it is a factor of 6.

HABITS OF MIND

Generalize Will the strategy you used to prove each statement work in proving other conditional statements?

Do You UNDERSTAND?

1. ESSENTIAL QUESTION What can you conclude when valid reasoning leads to a contradiction?

2. **Vocabulary** What are teh two types of indirect proof? How are they similar and how are they different?

3. **Error Analysis** Consider the figure below.

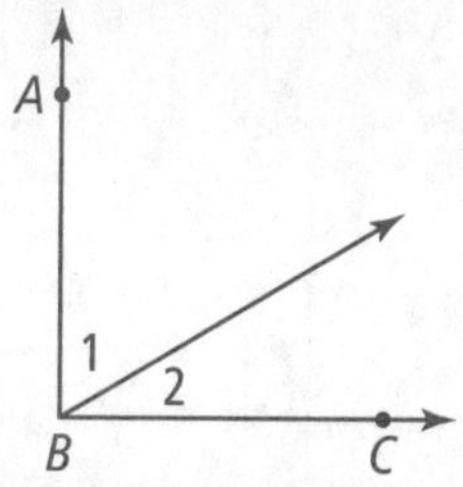

Consider the following conditional.

If $\angle ABC$ is a right angle and $m\angle 1 < 60$, then $m\angle 2 > 30$.

A student will prove the contrapositive as a way of proving the conditional. The student plans to assume $m\angle 2 < 30$ and then prove $m\angle 1 > 60$. Explain the error in the student's plan.

4. **Make Sense and Persevere** How do truth tables explain why proving the contrapositive also prove the original conditional statement?

5. **Generalize** Explain how you can identify the statement you assume and the statement you try to prove when writing a proof by contrapositive.

Do You KNOW HOW?

Use indirect reasoning to draw a conclusion in each situation.

6. Tamira only cuts the grass on a day that it does not rain. She cut the grass on Thursday.

7. Gabriela works at the library every Saturday morning. She did not work at the library this morning.

Write the first step of an indirect proof for each of the following statements.

8. $m\angle JKM = m\angle JKL - m\angle MKL$

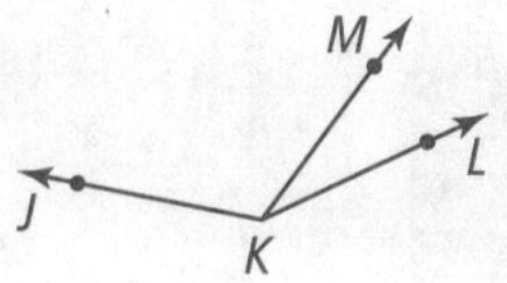

9. $\overline{PQ}$ is perpendicular to $\overline{ST}$.

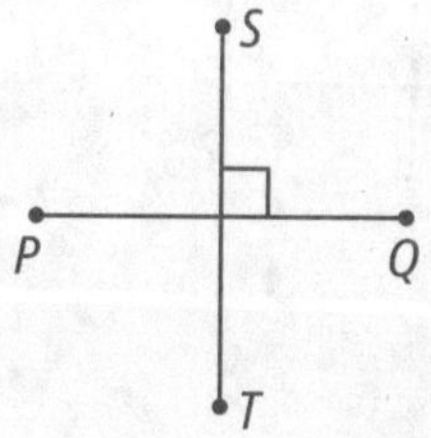

10. What can you conclude from the following situation using indirect reasoning? Explain.

- Nadeem spent more than \$10 but less than \$11 for a sandwich and drink.
- He spent \$8.49 on his sandwich.
- The cost for milk is \$1.49.
- The cost for orange juice is \$2.49.
- The cost for a tropical smoothie is \$2.89.
- The cost for apple juice is \$2.59.

Activity

7-1
Parallel Lines

SavvasRealize.com

EXPLORE & REASON

The diagram shows two parallel lines cut by a transversal.

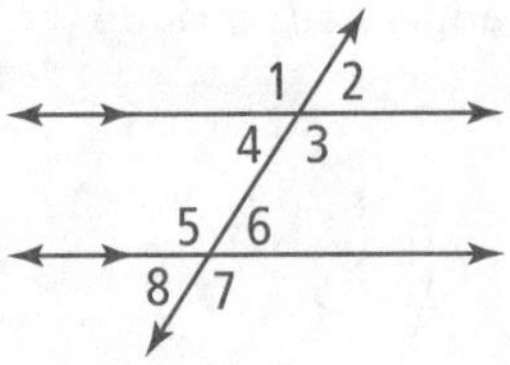

A. **Look for Relationships** What relationships among the measures of the angles do you see?

B. Suppose a different transversal intersects the parallel lines. Would you expect to find the same relationships in the measures of those angles? Explain.

HABITS OF MIND

Look for Relationships What theorems have you already learned that can be used to show why some of the angles formed are congruent?

EXAMPLE 1

Try It! Identify Angle Pairs

1. Which angle pairs include the named angle?

   a. $\angle 4$

   b. $\angle 7$

EXAMPLE 2

Try It! Explore Angle Relationships

2. If $m\angle 4 = 118°$, what is the measure of each of the other angles?

EXAMPLE 3

Try It! Prove the Alternate Interior Angles Theorem

3. Prove the Corresponding Angles Theorem.

   Given: $m \parallel n$

   Prove: $\angle 1 \cong \angle 2$

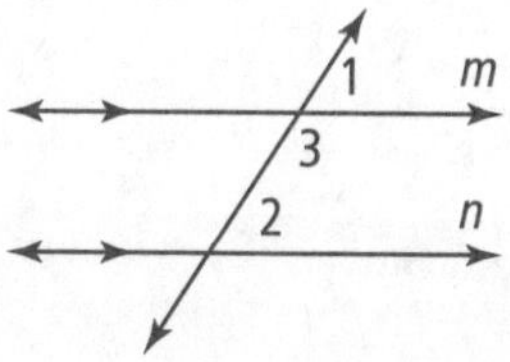

HABITS OF MIND

Generalize Suppose that a transversal intersects a pair of parallel lines, and one of the angles created measures *x*. What must be true of the other interior angles that are formed?

Assess

EXAMPLE 4

Try It! Use Parallel Lines to Prove an Angle Relationship

4. Given $\overline{AB} \parallel \overline{CD}$, prove that $m\angle 1 + m\angle 2 + m\angle 3 = 180$.

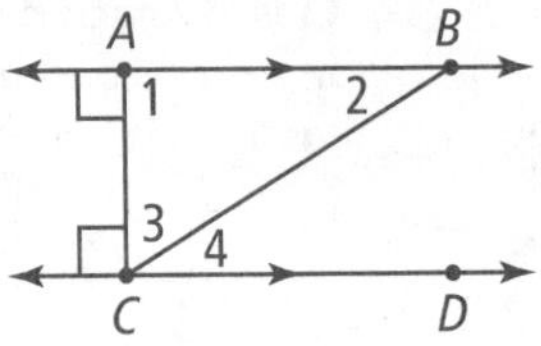

EXAMPLE 5

Try It! Find Angle Measures

5. If $m\angle EJF = 56$, find $m\angle FHK$.

HABITS OF MIND

Make Sense and Persevere What are some strategies you can use to find unknown angle measures?

Do You UNDERSTAND?

1. ESSENTIAL QUESTION What angle relationships are created when parallel lines are intersected by a transversal?

2. **Vocabulary** When a transversal intersects two parallel lines, which angle pairs are congruent?

3. **Error Analysis** What error did Leah make?

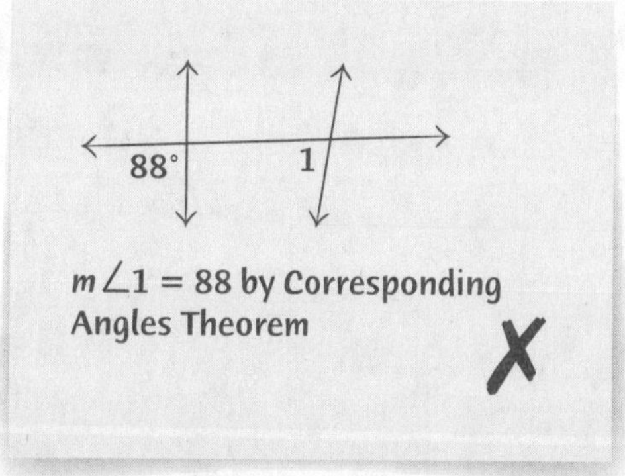

4. **Generalize** For any pair of angles formed by a transversal intersecting parallel lines, what are two possible relationships?

Do You KNOW HOW?

Use the diagram for Exercises 5–8.

Classify each pair of angles. Compare angle measures and give the postulate or theorem that justifies it.

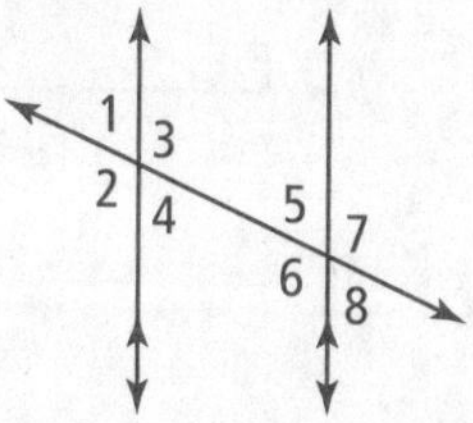

5. $\angle 2$ and $\angle 6$

6. $\angle 3$ and $\angle 5$

If $m\angle 1 = 71$, find the measure of each angle.

7. $\angle 5$

8. $\angle 7$

9. Elm St. and Spruce St. are parallel. What is $m\angle 1$?

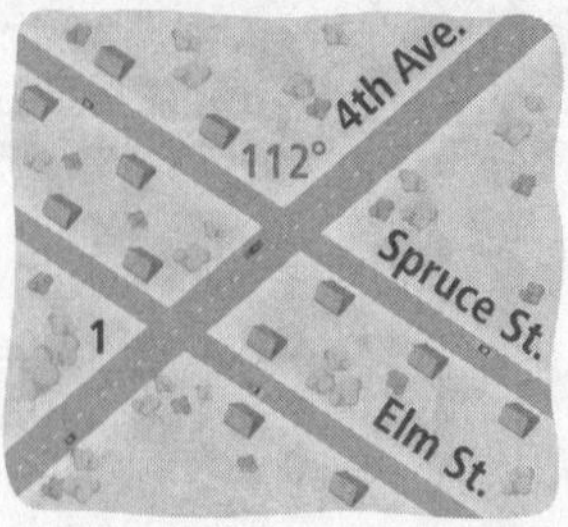

Activity

7-2 Proving Lines Parallel

SavvasRealize.com

CRITIQUE & EXPLAIN

Juan analyzes the diagram to see if line ℓ is parallel to line m. His teacher asks if there is enough information to say whether the lines are parallel.

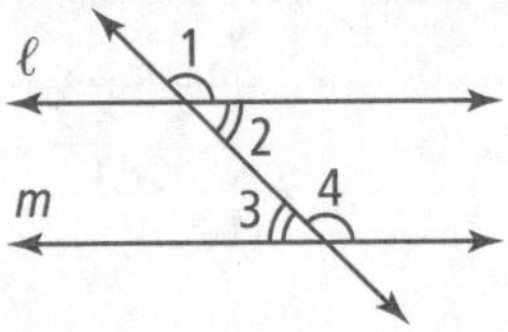

Yes, if a transversal intersects two parallel lines, then alternate interior angles are congruent and corresponding angles are congruent. I have both angle relationships here, so the lines are parallel.

A. Make Sense and Persevere Why is Juan's statement correct or incorrect?

B. Can you use the Alternate Exterior Angles Theorem to prove that the lines are not parallel?

HABITS OF MIND

Make Sense and Persevere Would Juan's statement be correct if he had referred to corresponding angles instead of alternate interior angles? Explain.

Notes

Assess

EXAMPLE 1

Try It! Understand Angle Relationships

1. Could $\angle 3$ be supplementary to a 120° angle? Explain.

EXAMPLE 2

Try It! Write a Flow Proof of Theorem 2-5

2. Write a flow proof for Theorem 2-6, the Converse of the Same-Side Interior Angles Postulate.

HABITS OF MIND

Construct Arguments How do you decide which statements to start with when writing a flow proof?

Notes

Assess

EXAMPLE 3

Try It! Determine Whether Lines Are Parallel

3. What is $m\angle 1$? What should $\angle 2$ measure in order to guarantee that the sidewalk is parallel to Main Street? Explain.

EXAMPLE 4

Try It! Solve a Problem With Parallel Lines

4. a. Bailey needs board *c* to be parallel to board *a*. What should $\angle 2$ measure? Explain.

   b. Is $b \parallel c$? Explain.

HABITS OF MIND

Make Sense and Persevere When using angles formed by a transversal to prove that two lines are parallel, how do you decide which pair of angles to use in your proof?

Assess

Do You UNDERSTAND?

1. ESSENTIAL QUESTION What angle relationships can be used to prove that two lines intersected by a transversal are parallel?

2. **Error Analysis** Noemi wrote, "If $\angle 1 \cong \angle 2$, then by the Converse of the Same-Side Interior Angles Postulate, $\ell \parallel m$." Explain the error in Noemi's reasoning.

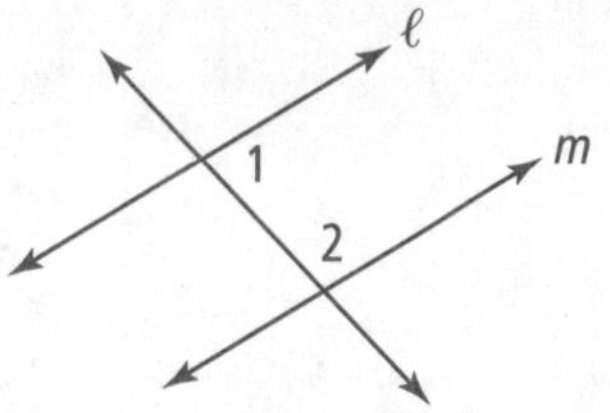

3. **Vocabulary** How does a *flow proof* show logical steps in the proof of a conditional statement?

4. **Reason** How is Theorem 2-9 a special case of the Converse of the Corresponding Angles Theorem?

Do You KNOW HOW?

Use the figure shown for Exercises 5 and 6.

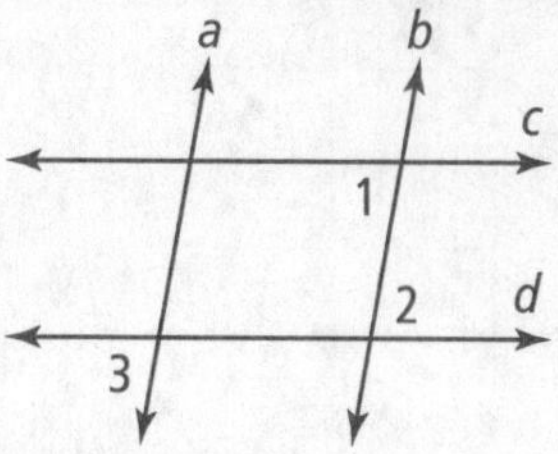

5. If $\angle 1 \cong \angle 2$, which theorem proves that $c \parallel d$?

6. If $m\angle 2 = 4x - 6$ and $m\angle 3 = 2x + 18$, for what value of x is $a \parallel b$? Which theorem justifies your answer?

7. Using the Converse of the Same-Side Interior Angles Postulate, what equation shows that $g \parallel h$?

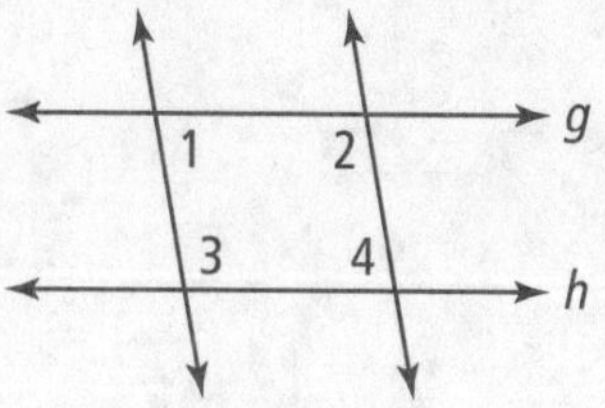

Activity

7-3 Parallel Lines and Triangle Angle Sums

SavvasRealize.com

EXPLORE & REASON

Two parallel lines never intersect. But, can two lines that intersect ever be parallel to the same line?

Draw point *P*. Then draw lines *a* and *b* that intersect at point *P* as shown.

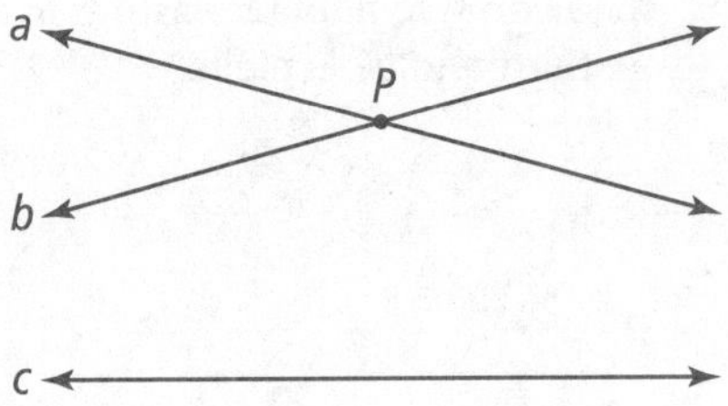

A. Place a pencil below the intersecting lines on your paper to represent line *c*. Rotate the pencil so that it is parallel to line *b*. Can you rotate the pencil so that it is parallel to line *a* at the same time?

B. Look for Relationships Can you adjust your drawing of the two intersecting lines so you can rotate the pencil to be parallel to both lines?

HABITS OF MIND

Look for Relationships Suppose you draw two lines that are parallel. Is it possible to draw a third line that intersects only one of the parallel lines? Explain.

Assess

EXAMPLE 1

Try It! Investigate the Measures of Triangle Angles

1. Given two angle measures in a triangle, can you find the measure of the third angle? Explain.

EXAMPLE 2

Try It! Prove the Triangle Angle-Sum Theorem

2. How does Theorem 2-10 justify the construction of the line through C that is parallel to $\overleftrightarrow{AB}$?

EXAMPLE 3

Try It! Use the Triangle Angle-Sum Theorem

3. What are the values of x and y in each figure?

a.

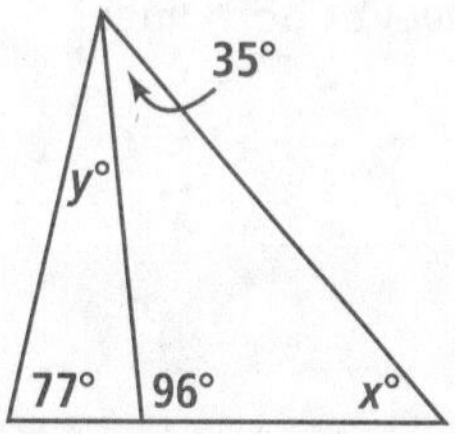

b.

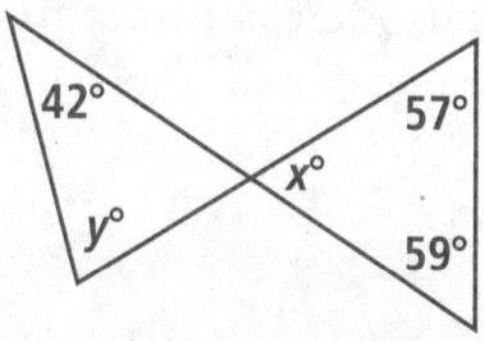

HABITS OF MIND

Reason When applying the Angle Sum Postulate in the Triangle Angle-Sum Theorem, how do you know that the sum of the angle measures is 180°?

Assess

EXAMPLE 4 **Try It!** **Apply the Triangle Exterior Angle Theorem**

4. What is the value of x in each figure?

a.

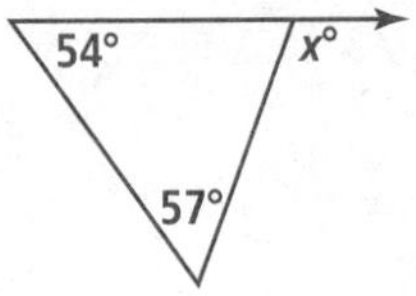

b.

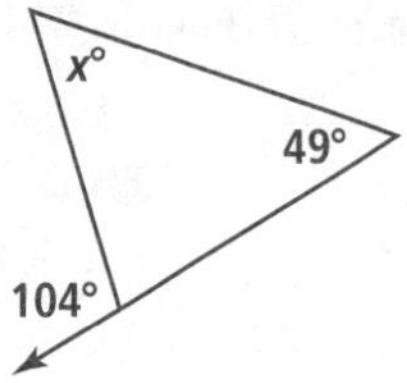

EXAMPLE 5 **Try It!** **Apply the Triangle Theorems**

5. What are the measures of ∠4 and ∠5? Explain.

HABITS OF MIND

Look for Relationships How is the Triangle Exterior Angle Theorem related to the Triangle Angle-Sum Theorem?

Do You UNDERSTAND?

1. ESSENTIAL QUESTION What is true about the interior and exterior angle measures of any triangle?

2. **Error Analysis** Chiang determined that the value of x is 103 and the value of y is 132 in the figure below. What mistake did Chiang make?

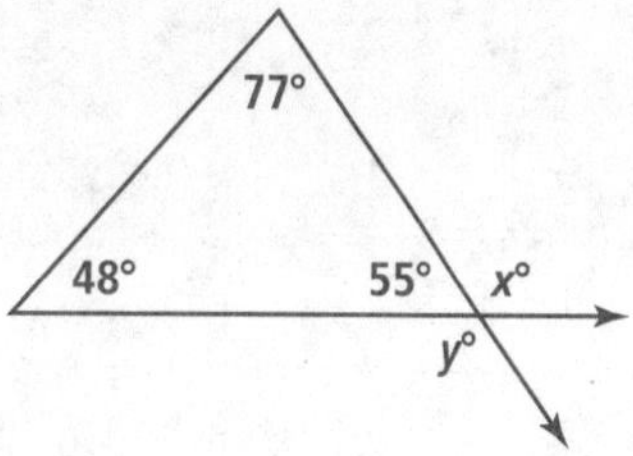

3. **Vocabulary** The word *remote* means distant or far apart. What parts of a figure are *remote interior angles* distant from?

4. **Look for Relationships** Use the Triangle Angle-Sum Theorem to answer the following questions. Explain your answers.
   a. What are the measures of each angle of an equiangular triangle?
   b. If one of the angle measures of an isosceles triangle is 90, what are the measures of the other two angles?

Do You KNOW HOW?

What is the value of x in each figure?

5.

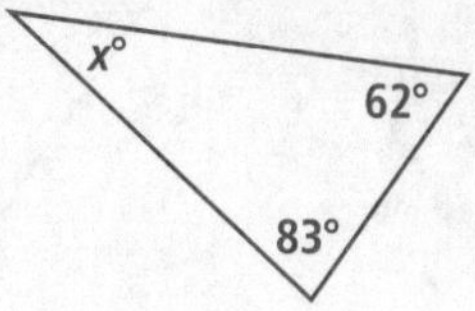

6.

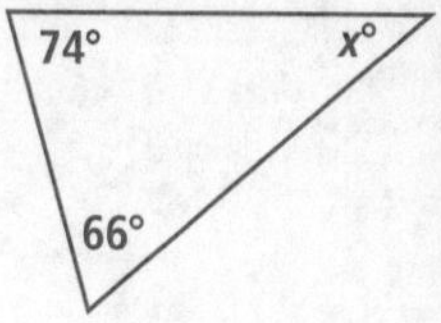

What is the value of x in each figure?

7.

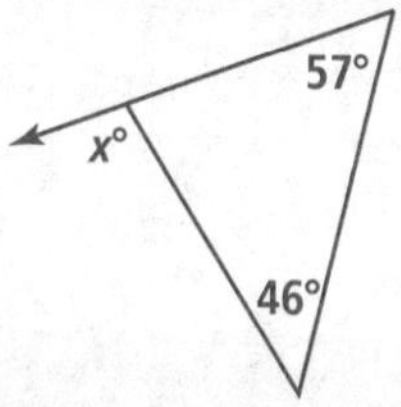

8.

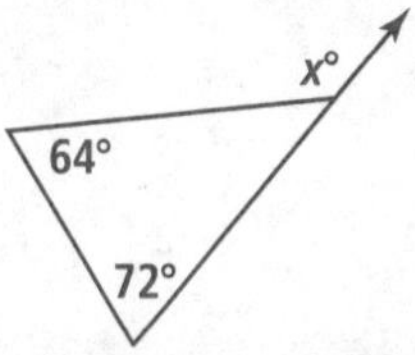

9. Write an equation relating the measures of $\angle 1$, $\angle 2$, and $\angle 3$. Write another equation relating the measures of $\angle 1$, $\angle 2$, and $\angle 4$.

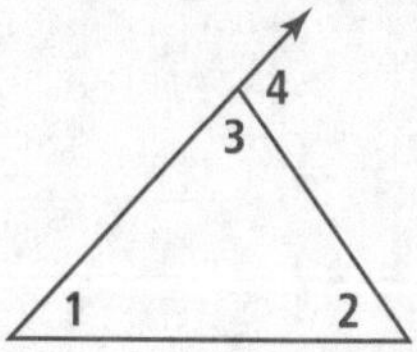

MODEL & DISCUSS

Pilar and Jake begin climbing to the top of a 100-ft monument at the same time along two different sets of steps at the same rate. The tables show their distances above ground level after a number of steps.

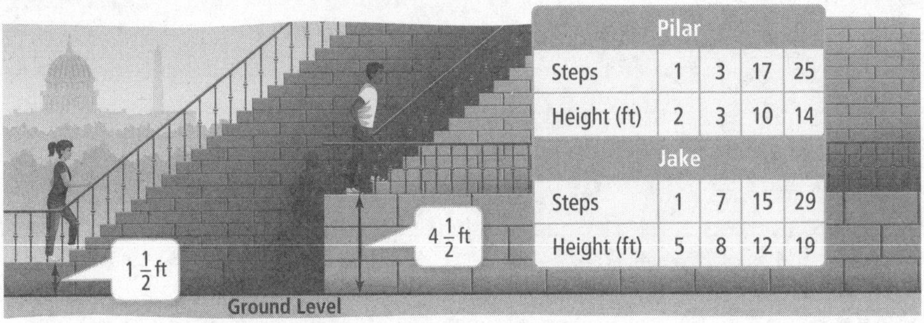

Pilar				
Steps	1	3	17	25
Height (ft)	2	3	10	14

Jake				
Steps	1	7	15	29
Height (ft)	5	8	12	19

A. How many feet does each student climb after 10 steps? Explain.

B. Will Pilar and Jake be at the same height after the same number of steps? Explain.

C. Reason What would you expect the graphs of each to look like given your answers to parts A and B? Explain.

HABITS OF MIND

Model With Mathematics What would it mean if the graphs intersected?

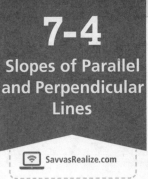

Notes

Assess

EXAMPLE 1

Try It! Slopes of Parallel Lines

1. Suppose another line for a chair lift is placed at a constant distance c below the gondola line. What is an equation of the new line? Is the new line also parallel to the hill? Explain.

EXAMPLE 2

Try It! Check Parallelism

2. Are lines m and q parallel?

HABITS OF MIND

Reason Could two lines that are parallel ever pass through the same point?

EXAMPLE 3

Try It! Check Perpendicularity

3. a. Are lines h and ℓ perpendicular?

b. Are lines k and m perpendicular?

EXAMPLE 4

Try It! Write Equations of Parallel and Perpendicular Lines

4. What are equations of lines parallel and perpendicular to the given line k passing through point T?

a. $y = -3x + 2$; $T(3, 1)$

b. $y = \frac{3}{4}x - 5$; $T(12, -2)$

HABITS OF MIND

Generalize How can you use slope to determine if two lines are perpendicular, parallel, or neither perpendicular or parallel?

Do You UNDERSTAND?

1. **ESSENTIAL QUESTION** How do the slopes of the lines that are parallel to each other compare? How do the slopes of the lines that are perpendicular to each other compare?

2. **Error Analysis** Katrina said that the lines $y = -\frac{2}{3}x + 5$ and $y = -\frac{3}{2}x + 2$ are perpendicular. Explain Katrina's error.

3. **Reason** Give an equation for a line perpendicular to the line $y = 0$. Is there more than one such line? Explain.

4. **Communicate Precisely** What are two different if-then statements implied by Theorem 2-13?

5. **Error Analysis** Devin said that $\overleftrightarrow{AB}$ and $\overleftrightarrow{CD}$ for $A(-2, 0)$, $B(2, 3)$, $C(1, -1)$, and $D(5, -4)$ are parallel. Explain and correct Devin's error.

> slope of $\overleftrightarrow{AB}$: $\frac{3-0}{2-(-2)} = \frac{3}{4}$
>
> slope of $\overleftrightarrow{CD}$: $\frac{-1-(-4)}{5-1} = \frac{3}{4}$
>
> slopes are equal, so $\overleftrightarrow{AB} \parallel \overleftrightarrow{CD}$ ✗

Do You KNOW HOW?

Use the diagram for Exercises 6–9.

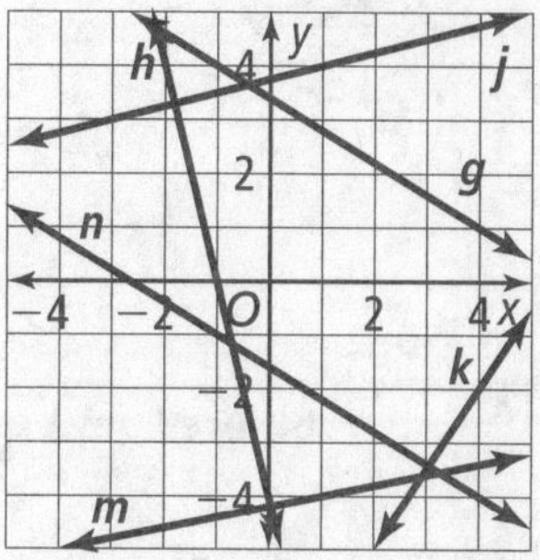

6. Are lines g and n parallel?

7. Are lines j and m parallel?

8. Are lines n and k perpendicular?

9. Are lines h and j perpendicular?

10. What is an equation for the line parallel to $y = -x + 7$ that passes through $(7, -2)$?

11. What is an equation for the line perpendicular to $y = 3x - 1$ that passes through $(-9, -2)$?

12. The graph of a roller coaster track goes in a straight line through coordinates (10, 54) and (42, 48), with coordinates in feet. A support beam runs parallel 12 feet below the track. What equation describes the support beam?

Video

MATHEMATICAL MODELING IN 3 ACTS

SavvasRealize.com

Parallel Paving Company

Building roads consists of many different tasks. Once civil engineers have designed the road, they work with surveyors and construction crews to clear and level the land. Sometimes specialists have to blast away rock in order to clear the land. Once the land is leveled, the crews bring in asphalt pavers to smooth out the hot asphalt.

Sometimes construction crews will start work at both ends of the new road and meet in the middle. Think about this during the Mathematical Modeling in 3 Acts lesson.

ACT 1 Identify the Problem

1. What is the first question that comes to mind after watching the video?

2. Write down the Main Question you will answer.

3. Make an initial conjecture that answers this Main Question.

4. Explain how you arrived at your conjecture.

5. What information will be useful to know to answer the main question? How can you get it? How will you use that information?

Video

ACT 2 Develop a Model

6. Use the math that you have learned in the topic to refine your conjecture.

ACT 3 Interpret the Results

7. Did your refined conjecture match the actual answer exactly? If not, what might explain the difference?

Activity

8-1 Reflections

SavvasRealize.com

EXPLORE & REASON

The illustration shows irregular pentagon-shaped tiles covering a floor.

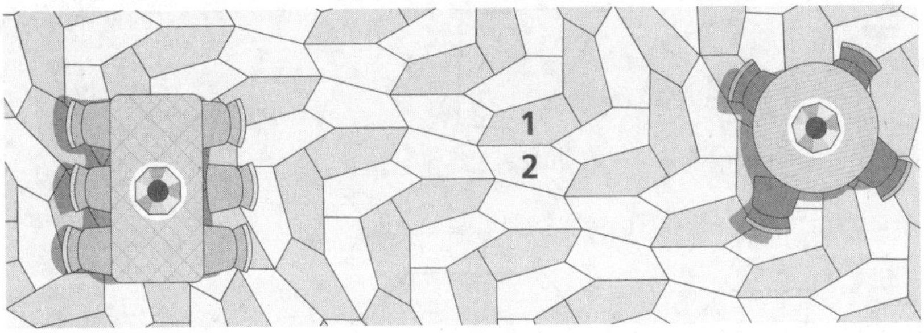

A. Which tiles are copies of tile 1? Explain.

B. Communicate Precisely If you were to move tile 1 from the design, what would you have to do so it completely covers tile 2?

C. Which tiles are *not* copies of tile 1? Explain.

HABITS OF MIND

Use Structure What patterns do you see in how the tiles cover the floor?

Assess

EXAMPLE 1

Try It! Identify Rigid Motions

1. Is each transformation a rigid motion? Explain.

a.

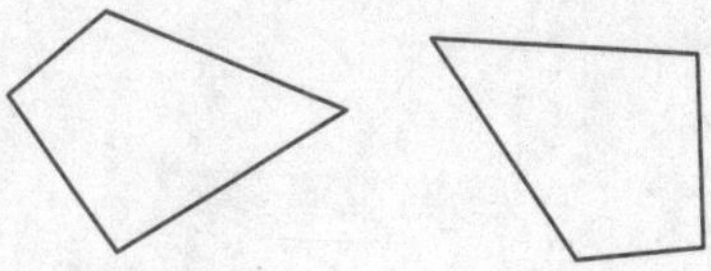

b.

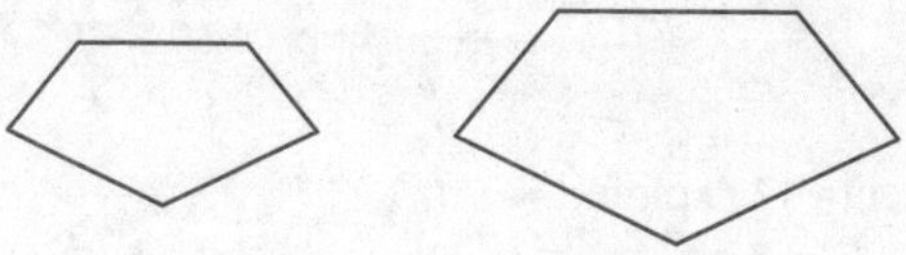

HABITS OF MIND

Construct Arguments What kind of evidence would you give to show that a transformation is not a rigid motion?

EXAMPLE 2

Try It! Reflect a Triangle Across a Line

2. What is the reflection of triangle $\triangle LMN$ across line n?

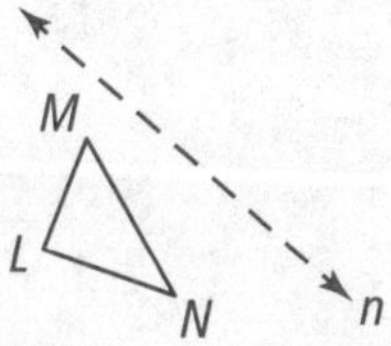

EXAMPLE 3

Try It! Reflect a Figure on a Coordinate Plane

3. Triangle ABC has vertices $A(-5, 6)$, $B(1, -2)$, and $C(-3, -4)$. What are the coordinates of the vertices of $\triangle A'B'C'$ for each reflection?

a. $R_{x\text{-axis}}$

b. $R_{y\text{-axis}}$

Notes

EXAMPLE 4

Try It! Describe a Reflection on the Coordinate Plane

4. What is a reflection rule that maps each triangle to its image?

   a. $C(3, 8)$, $D(5, 12)$, $E(4, 6)$ and $C'(-8, -3)$, $D'(-12, -5)$, $E'(-6, -4)$

   b. $F(7, 6)$, $G(0, -4)$, $H(-5, 0)$ and $F'(-5, 6)$, $G'(2, -4)$, $H'(7, 0)$

HABITS OF MIND

Reason What is the relationship between a preimage point to the line of reflection and its image point to the line of reflection?

EXAMPLE 5

Try It! Use Reflections

5. Student *A* sees the reflected image across the mirror of another student who appears to be at *B'*. Trace the diagram and show the actual position of Student *B*.

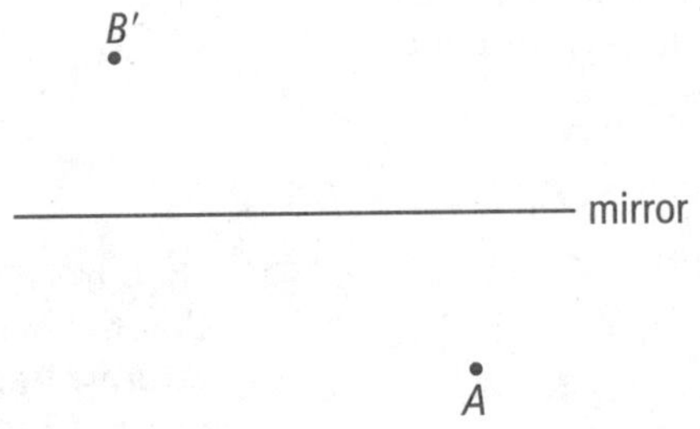

HABITS OF MIND

Make Sense and Persevere What is the relationship between an image you see in a mirror and the actual image?

Assess

Do You UNDERSTAND?

1. **ESSENTIAL QUESTION** How are the properties of reflection used to transform a figure?

2. **Error Analysis** Oscar drew the image of a triangle reflected across the line $y = -1$. What mistake did Oscar make?

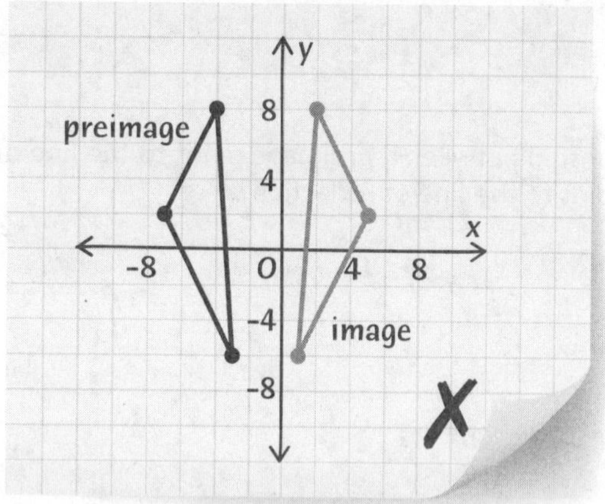

3. **Vocabulary** One meaning of the word *rigid* is "not bendable," and another is "unable to be changed." How do those meanings correspond to the definition of rigid motion?

4. **Communicate Precisely** How can you determine whether the transformation of a figure is a rigid motion?

5. **Generalize** Describe the steps you must take to identify the path an object will follow if it bounces off a surface and strikes another object.

Do You KNOW HOW?

6. Does the transformation appear to be a rigid motion? Explain.

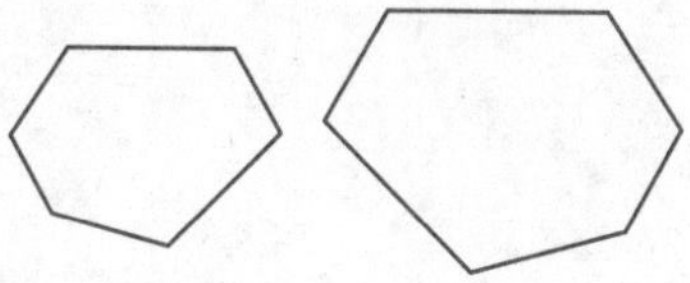

What are the coordinates of each image?

7. $R_{x\text{-axis}}(-5, 3)$

8. $R_{x\text{-axis}}(1, 6)$

9. Write a reflection rule for each triangle and its image.
   a. $J(1, 0)$, $K(-5, 2)$, $L(4, -4)$ and $J'(-9, 0)$, $K'(-3, 2)$, $L'(-12, -4)$
   b. $P(8, 6)$, $Q(-4, 12)$, $R(7, 7)$ and $P'(8, -20)$, $Q'(-4, -26)$, $R'(7, -21)$

10. Squash is a racket sport like tennis, except that the ball must bounce off a wall between returns. Trace the squash court. At what point on the front wall should player 1 aim at in order to reach the rear wall as far from player 2 as possible?

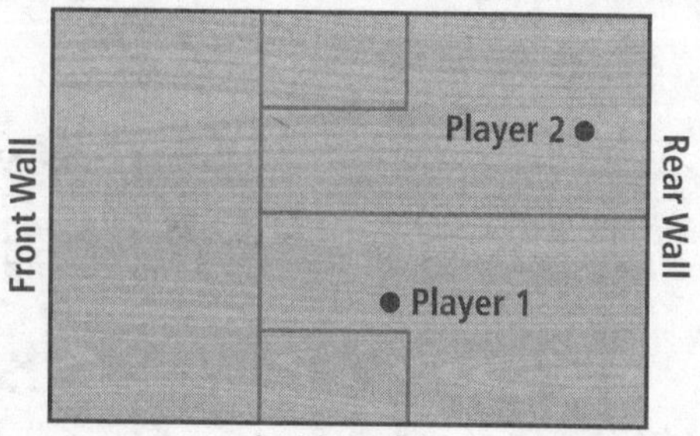

(not to scale)

Activity

8-2 Translations

SavvasRealize.com

EXPLORE & REASON

Draw a copy of *ABCD* on a grid. Using another color, draw a copy of *ABCD* on the grid in a different location with the same orientation, and label it *QRST*.

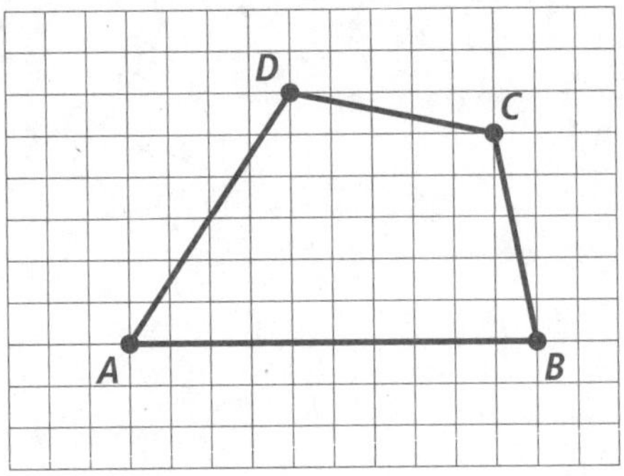

A. On another sheet of paper, write instructions that describe how to move *ABCD* to the location of *QRST*.

B. Exchange instructions with a partner. Follow your partner's instructions to draw a third shape *EFGH* in another color on the same grid. Compare your drawings. Do your drawings look the same? Explain.

C. Communicate Precisely What makes a set of instructions for this Explore & Reason a good set of instructions?

HABITS OF MIND

Use Appropriate Tools Why is placing the figures on a grid helpful in writing a set of instructions?

EXAMPLE 1

Try It! Find the Image of a Translation

1. What are the vertices of $\triangle E'F'G'$ produced by each translation?

   a. $T_{\langle 6, -7 \rangle}(\triangle EFG) = \triangle E'F'G'$

   b. $T_{\langle 11, 2 \rangle}(\triangle EFG) = \triangle E'F'G'$

EXAMPLE 2

Try It! Write a Translation Rule

2. What translation rule maps $P(-3, 1)$ to its image $P'(2, 3)$?

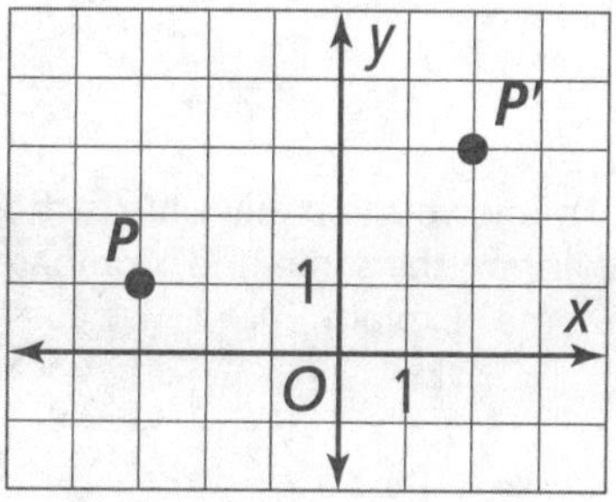

HABITS OF MIND

Communicate Precisely For Examples 1 and 2, how might you explain what it means to move the same distance and in the same direction?

Assess

EXAMPLE 3

Try It! Compose Translations

3. What is the composition of the transformations written as one transformation?

a. $T_{\langle 3, -2 \rangle} \circ T_{\langle 1, -1 \rangle}$

b. $T_{\langle -4, 0 \rangle} \circ T_{\langle -2, 5 \rangle}$

HABITS OF MIND

Use Structure What do you notice about the order of composing two translations?

EXAMPLE 4

Try It! Relate Translations and Reflections

4. Suppose n is the line with equation $y = 1$. Given $\triangle DEF$ with vertices $D(0, 0)$, $E(0, 3)$, and $F(3, 0)$, what translation image is equivalent to $(R_n \circ R_{x\text{-axis}})(\triangle DEF)$?

EXAMPLE 5

Try It! Prove Theorem 3-1

5. Suppose the point B you chose in the Proof of Theorem 3-1 was between lines m and n. How would that affect the proof? What are the possible cases you need to consider?

HABITS OF MIND

Make Sense and Persevere When you want to choose two reflections to make a translation, what do you notice about the first line of reflection you choose?

Do You UNDERSTAND?

1. ESSENTIAL QUESTION What are the properties of a translation?

2. **Error Analysis** Sasha says that for any $\triangle XYZ$, the reflection over the y-axis composed with the reflection over the x-axis is equivalent to a translation of $\triangle XYZ$. Explain Sasha's error.

3. **Vocabulary** Write an example of a composition of rigid motions for $\triangle PQR$.

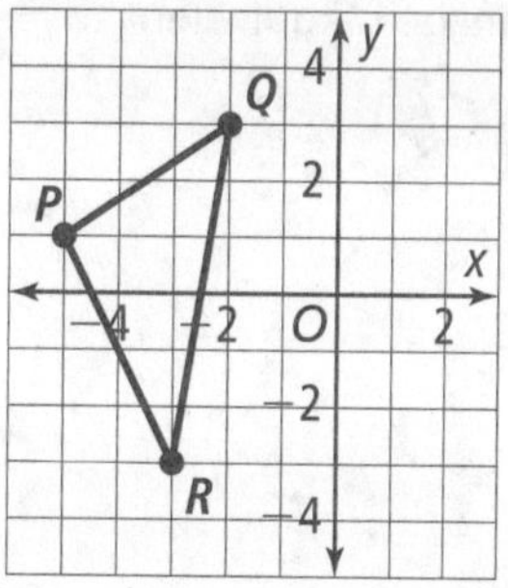

4. **Make Sense and Persevere** What are the values of x and y if $T_{\langle -2, 7\rangle}(x, y) = (3, -1)$?

Do You KNOW HOW?

For Exercises 5 and 6, the vertices of $\triangle XYZ$ are $X(1, -4)$, $Y(-2, -1)$, and $Z(3, 1)$. For each translation, give the vertices of $\triangle X'Y'Z'$.

5. $T_{\langle -4, -2\rangle}(\triangle XYZ)$

6. $T_{\langle 5, -3\rangle}(\triangle XYZ)$

7. What is the rule for the translation shown?

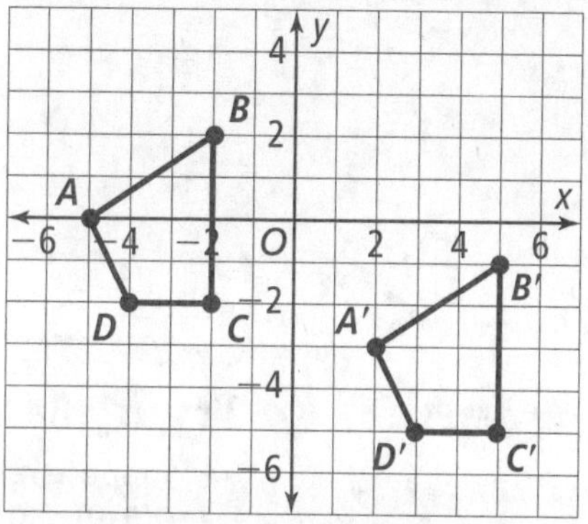

For Exercises 8 and 9, write the composition of translations as one translation.

8. $T_{\langle 7, 8\rangle} \circ T_{\langle -3, -4\rangle}$

9. $T_{\langle 0, 3\rangle} \circ T_{\langle 4, 6\rangle}$

10. How far apart are two parallel lines m and n such that $T_{\langle 12, 0\rangle}(\triangle JKL) = (R_n \circ R_m)(\triangle JKL)$?

Activity

8-3 Rotations

SavvasRealize.com

CRITIQUE & EXPLAIN

Fllipe says that the next time one of the hands of the clock points to 7 will be at 7:00 when the hour hand points to 7. Nadia says that it will be at 5:35 when the minute hand points to 7.

A. Whose statement is correct? Explain.

B. Communicate Precisely Suppose the numbers on the clock face are removed. Write instructions that another person could follow to move the minute hand from 2 to 6.

HABITS OF MIND

Generalize How are rotating and translating a figure alike? How are they different?

Assess

EXAMPLE 1

Try It! Draw a Rotated Image

1. Do you think a rotated image would ever coincide with the original figure? Explain.

EXAMPLE 2

Try It! Draw Rotations in the Coordinate Plane

2. The vertices of $\triangle XYZ$ are $X(-4, 7)$, $Y(0, 8)$, and $Z(2, -1)$.
   a. What are the vertices of $r_{(180^\circ, O)}(\triangle XYZ)$?

   b. What are the vertices of $r_{(270^\circ, O)}(\triangle XYZ)$?

EXAMPLE 3

Try It! Use Rotations

3. a. Suppose the drumline instead turns counterclockwise about B'. How many degrees must it rotate so that the sixth drummer ends in the same position?

   b. Can the composition of rotations be described by $r_{(45^\circ, A)}$ since $180^\circ - 135^\circ = 45^\circ$? Explain.

HABITS OF MIND

Make Sense and Persevere What information do you need in order to find the image of one or more rotations?

Assess

EXAMPLE 4

Try It! Investigate Reflections and Rotations

4. Perform the same constructions shown, except draw line *p* so that it does not pass through *T*. Do you get the same results? Explain.

EXAMPLE 5

Try It! Prove Theorem 3-2

5. Suppose point *Q* is closer to point *B* or even outside of $\angle APB$. Does the relationship still hold for the angle between the reflection lines and the angle between the preimage and the image? Explain.

HABITS OF MIND

Use Structure What could you look for with two lines of reflection to see if the composition of reflections might result in a given rotation?

Do You UNDERSTAND?

1. ESSENTIAL QUESTION What are the properties that identify a rotation?

2. **Error Analysis** Isabel drew the diagram below to show the rotation of $\triangle DEF$ about point T. What is her error?

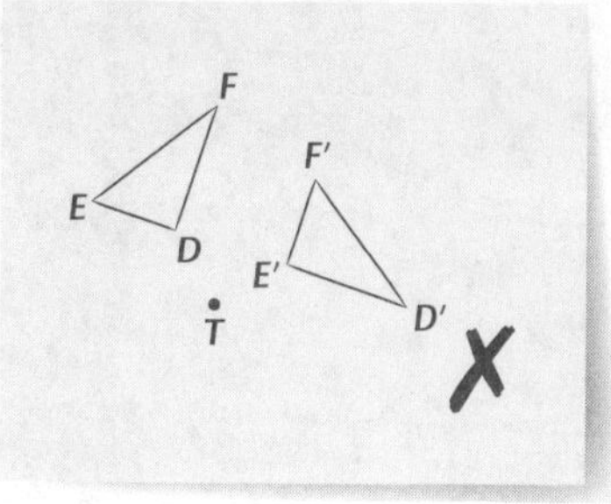

3. **Vocabulary** How is the *center of rotation* related to the *center of a circle*?

4. **Construct Arguments** In the diagram, $\triangle A''B''C''$ is the image of reflections of $\triangle ABC$ across lines p and q. It is also the image of a rotation of $\triangle ABC$ about R. What is the angle of rotation? Explain.

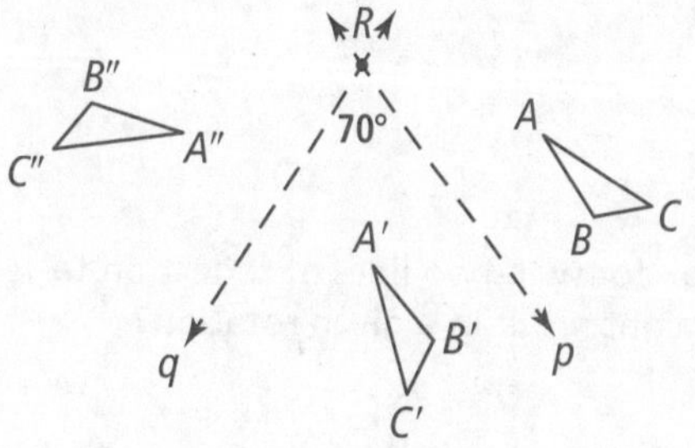

Do You KNOW HOW?

Trace each figure and draw its rotated image.

5. $r_{(90°, P)}(\overline{MN})$

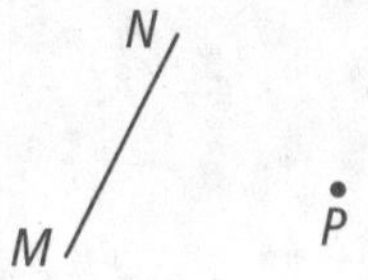

6. $r_{(120°, T)}(\triangle ABC)$

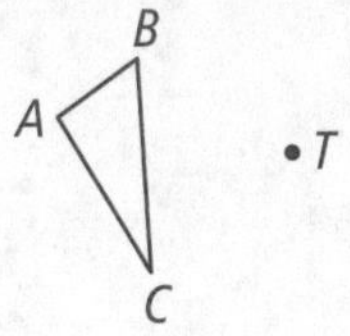

Give the coordinates of each image.

7. $r_{(180°, O)}(\overline{GH})$ for $G(2, -9)$, $H(-1, 3)$

8. $r_{(90°, O)}(\triangle XYZ)$ for $X(0, 3)$, $Y(1, -4)$, $Z(5, 2)$

Trace each figure and construct two lines of reflection such that the composition of the reflections across the lines maps onto the image shown.

9.

10.

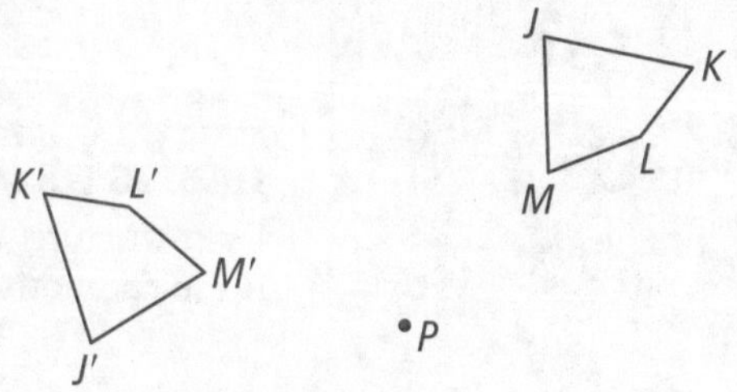

8-4 Classification of Rigid Motions

SavvasRealize.com

CRITIQUE & EXPLAIN

Two students are trying to determine whether compositions of rigid motions are commutative. Paula translates a triangle and then reflects it across a line. When she reflects and then translates, she gets the same image. She concludes that compositions of rigid motions are commutative.

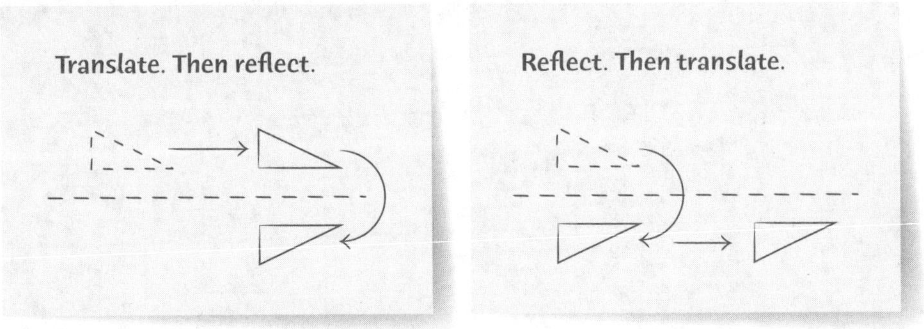

Keenan rotates a triangle and then reflects it. When he changes the order of the rigid motions, he gets a different image. He concludes that compositions of rigid motions are not commutative.

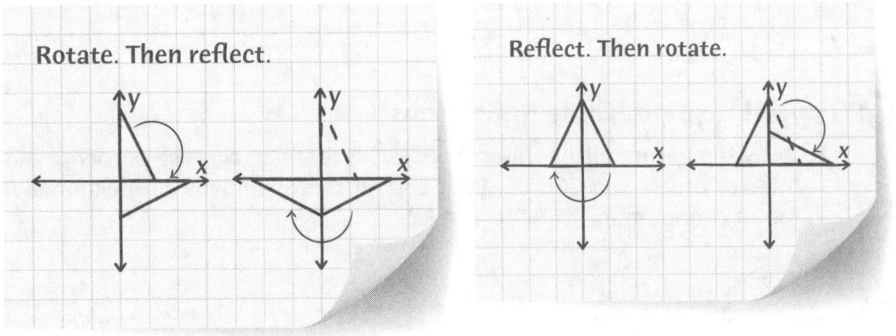

A. Should Paula have used grid paper? Explain.

B. Communicate Precisely Do you agree with Paula or with Keenan? Explain.

HABITS OF MIND

Communicate Precisely What should you look for to determine whether two given rigid motions are commutative?

Notes

Assess

EXAMPLE 1

Try It! Prove Theorem 3-3

1. Describe how you can use the reasoning used to prove Theorem 3-3 to show that the theorem is true when composing three rigid motions. Can your strategy be extended to include any number of rigid motions?

EXAMPLE 2

Try It! Explore Glide Reflections

2. Draw the perpendicular bisector of $\overline{BB'}$. Is that line also the perpendicular bisector of $\overline{AA'}$ and $\overline{CC'}$? Use your answer to explain why a reflection alone can or cannot map $\triangle ABC$ to $\triangle A'B'C'$.

HABITS OF MIND

Use Structure What observations do you make about a figure to determine the type of rigid motion?

Notes

Assess

EXAMPLE 3

Try It! Find the Image of a Glide Reflection

3. Quadrilateral *RSTV* has vertices $R(-3, 2)$, $S(0, 5)$, $T(4, -4)$, and $V(0, -2)$. Use the rule $T_{\langle 1, 0 \rangle} \circ R_{x\text{-axis}}$ to graph and label the glide reflection of *RSTV*.

EXAMPLE 4

Try It! Determine a Glide Reflection

4. What is the glide reflection that maps each of the following?

a. $\triangle ABC \rightarrow \triangle A'B'C'$ given $A(-3, 4)$, $B(-4, 2)$, $C(-1, 1)$, $A'(1, 1)$, $B'(2, -1)$, and $C'(-1, -2)$.

b. $\overline{RS} \rightarrow \overline{R'S'}$ given $R(-2, 4)$, $S(2, 6)$, $R'(4, 0)$, and $S'(8, -2)$.

HABITS OF MIND

Make Sense and Persevere What other strategy could you use to find a glide reflection?

Do You UNDERSTAND?

1. ESSENTIAL QUESTION How can rigid motions be classified?

2. Is it correct to say that the composition of a translation followed by a reflection is a glide reflection? Explain.

3. **Error Analysis** Tamika draws the following diagram as an example of a glide reflection. What error did she make?

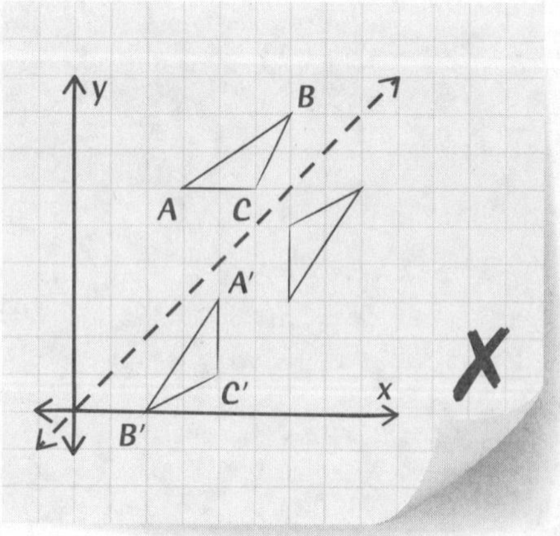

Do You KNOW HOW?

Use the figures for Exercises 4–7. Identify each rigid motion as a translation, a reflection, a rotation, or a glide reflection.

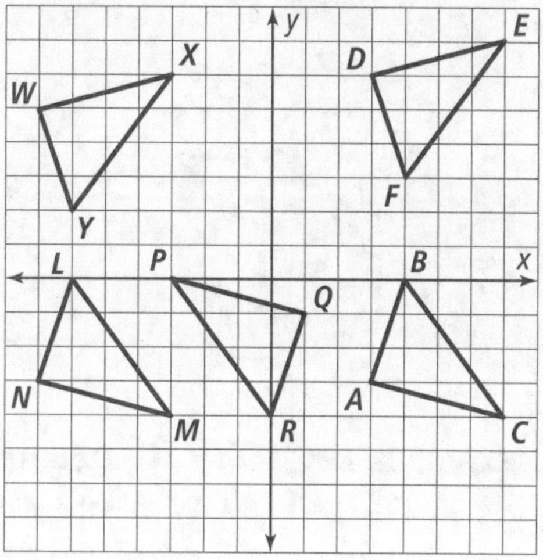

4. $\triangle WYX \rightarrow \triangle NLM$

5. $\triangle DFE \rightarrow \triangle WYX$

6. $\triangle WYX \rightarrow \triangle ABC$

7. $\triangle NLM \rightarrow \triangle QRP$

8-5 Symmetry

EXPLORE & REASON

Look at the kaleidoscope image shown. Then consider pieces A and B taken from the image.

A. How are piece A and piece B related? Describe a rigid motion that you can use on piece B to produce piece A.

B. Communicate Precisely Describe a composition of rigid motions that you can use on piece A to produce the image.

C. How many rigid motions did you need to produce the image from piece A? Can you think of another composition of rigid motions to produce the image starting with piece A?

HABITS OF MIND

Reason What part of the figure is piece A? How does that fraction relate to the number of rigid motions needed to produce the entire figure?

EXAMPLE 1

Try It! Identify Transformations for Symmetry

1. What transformations map each figure onto itself?

a.

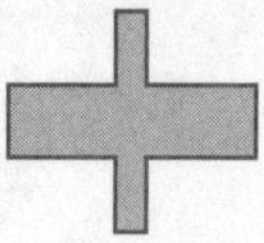

b.

EXAMPLE 2

Try It! Identify Lines of Symmetry

2. How many lines of symmetry does each figure have? How do you know whether you have found them all?

a.

b.

EXAMPLE 3

Try It! Identify Rotational Symmetry

3. What are the rotational symmetries for each figure? Does each figure have point symmetry?

a.

b.

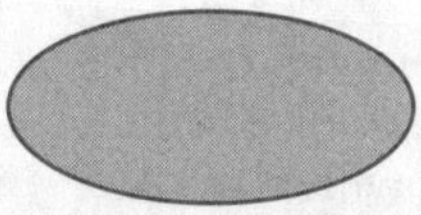

HABITS OF MIND

Use Structure How do you know if you have found all lines of symmetry to a figure?

Notes

Assess

EXAMPLE 4

Try It! Determine Symmetries

4. What symmetries does a square have?

EXAMPLE 5

Try It! Use Symmetry

5. What is a possible design for a circular logo that looks the same for each 60° rotation and uses at least two colors?

HABITS OF MIND

Make Sense and Persevere What steps can you take to determine if a figure has symmetry?

Do You UNDERSTAND?

1. ESSENTIAL QUESTION How can you tell whether a figure is symmetric?

2. **Error Analysis** For the figure below, Adam was asked to draw all lines of reflection. His work is shown. What error did Adam make?

3. **Vocabulary** What type of symmetry does a figure have if it can be mapped onto itself by being flipped over a line?

4. **Communicate Precisely** What does it mean for a figure to have 60° rotational symmetry?

5. **Construct Arguments** Is it possible for a figure to have rotational symmetry and no reflectional symmetry? Explain or give examples.

Do You KNOW HOW?

Find the number of lines of symmetry for each figure.

6. 

7. 

Describe the rotational symmetry of each figure. State whether each has point symmetry.

8. 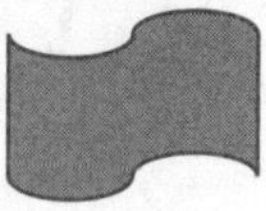

9. 

Identify the types of symmetry of each figure. For each figure with reflectional symmetry, identify the lines of symmetry. For each figure with rotational symmetry, identify the angles of rotation that map the figure onto itself.

10. 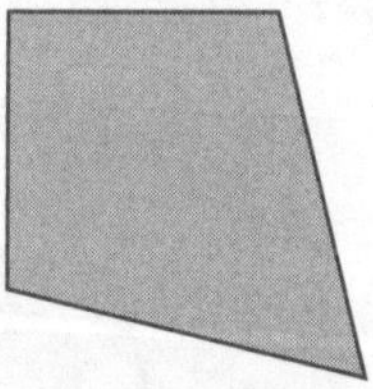

11. 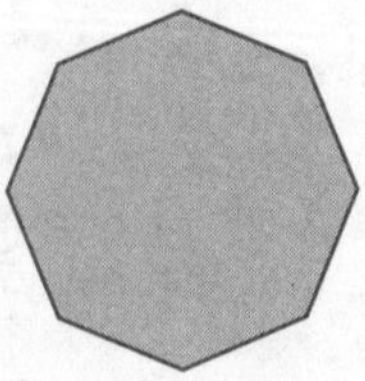

Video

MATHEMATICAL MODELING IN 3 ACTS

SavvasRealize.com

The Perplexing Polygon

Look around and you will see shapes and patterns everywhere you look. The tiles on a floor are often all the same shape and fit together to form a pattern. The petals on a flower often make a repeating pattern around the center of the flower. When you look at snowflakes under a microscope, you'll notice that they are made up of repeating three-dimensional crystals. Think about this during the Mathematical Modeling in 3 Acts lesson.

ACT 1 Identify the Problem

1. What is the first question that comes to mind after watching the video?

2. Write down the Main Question you will answer.

3. Make an initial conjecture that answers this Main Question.

4. Explain how you arrived at your conjecture.

5. What information will be useful to know to answer the main question? How can you get it? How will you use that information?

ACT 2 Develop a Model

6. Use the math that you have learned in the topic to refine your conjecture.

ACT 3 Interpret the Results

7. Did your refined conjecture match the actual answer exactly? If not, what might explain the difference?

Activity

SavvasRealize.com

EXPLORE & REASON

Some corporate logos are distinctive because they make use of repeated shapes.

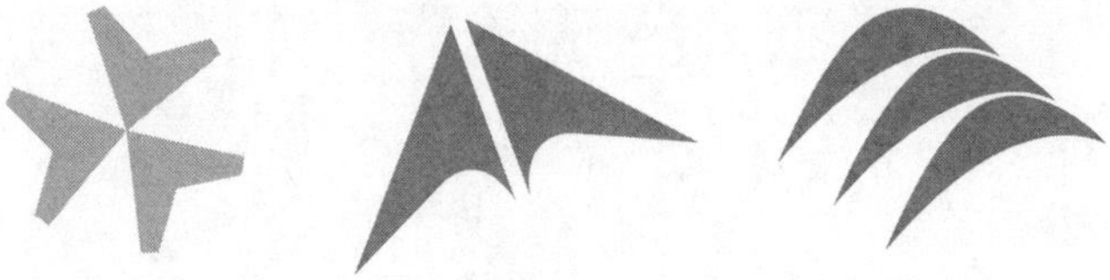

A designer creates two versions of a new logo for the Bolt Company. Version 1 uses the original image shown at the right and a reflection of it. Version 2 uses reduced copies of the original image.

A. Make a sketch of each version.

B. Communicate Precisely The owner of the company says, "I like your designs, but it is important that the transformed image be the same size and shape as the original image." What would you do to comply with the owner's requirements?

C. What transformations can you apply to the original image that would produce logos acceptable to the owner? Explain.

HABITS OF MIND

Use Structure Is comparing the measures of all the angles in a preimage and in an image sufficient to guarantee the figures are congruent?

Notes

Assess

EXAMPLE 1

Try It! Understand Congruence

1. A 90° rotation about the origin maps $\triangle PQR$ to $\triangle LMN$. Are the triangles congruent? Explain.

EXAMPLE 2

Try It! Verify Congruence

2. Use the graph shown.

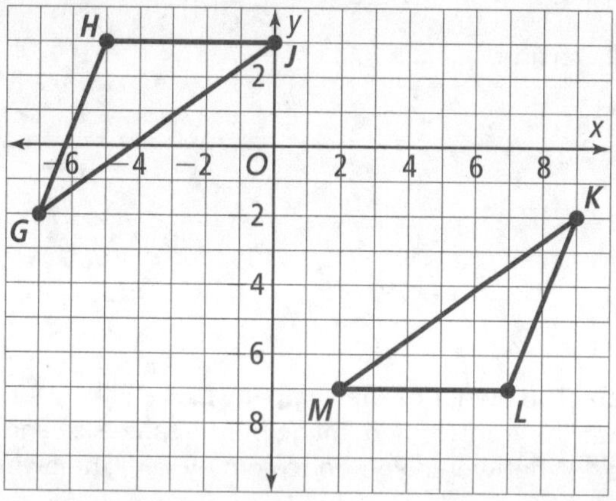

a. Given $\triangle GHJ \cong \triangle KLM$, what is one composition of rigid motions that maps $\triangle GHJ$ to $\triangle KLM$?

b. What is another composition of rigid motions that maps $\triangle GHJ$ to $\triangle KLM$?

HABITS OF MIND

Construct Arguments Can a figure be congruent to itself?

EXAMPLE 3 **Try It! Identify Congruent Figures**

3. Use the graph shown.

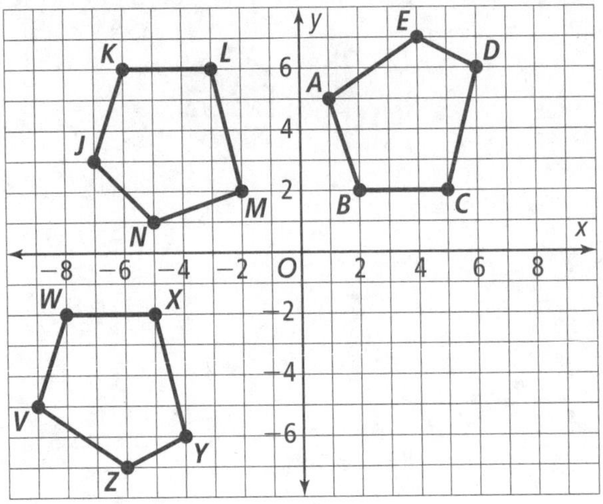

a. Are *ABCDE* and *JKLMN* congruent? If so, describe a composition of rigid motions that maps *ABCDE* to *JKLMN*. If not, explain.

b. Are *ABCDE* and *VWXYZ* congruent? If so, describe a composition of rigid motions that maps *ABCDE* to *VWXYZ*. If not, explain.

Notes

EXAMPLE 4

Try It! Determine Congruence

4. Is the pair of objects congruent? If so, describe a composition of rigid motions that maps one object onto the other.

a.

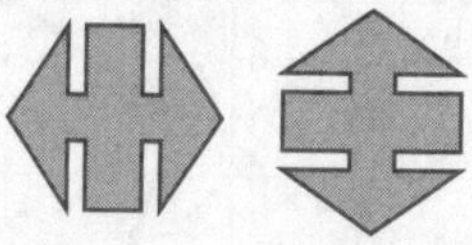

b.

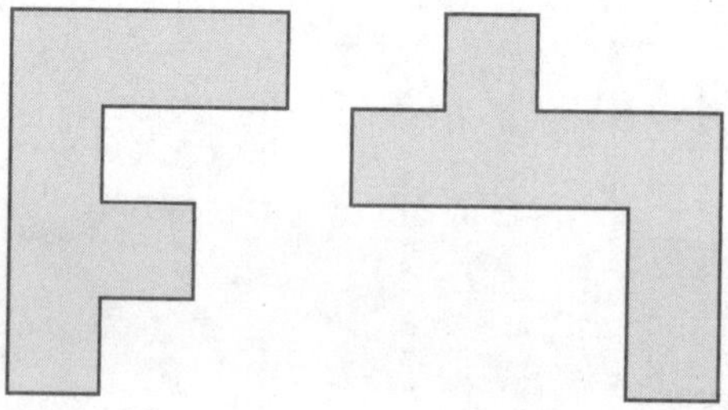

HABITS OF MIND

Use Structure If one part of an image is congruent to the corresponding part of the preimage, does that mean the entire image and preimage must be congruent?

Notes

Assess

EXAMPLE 5

Try It! Apply Congruence

5. Is Unit C congruent to Unit A? If so, describe the composition of rigid motions that maps Unit A to Unit C.

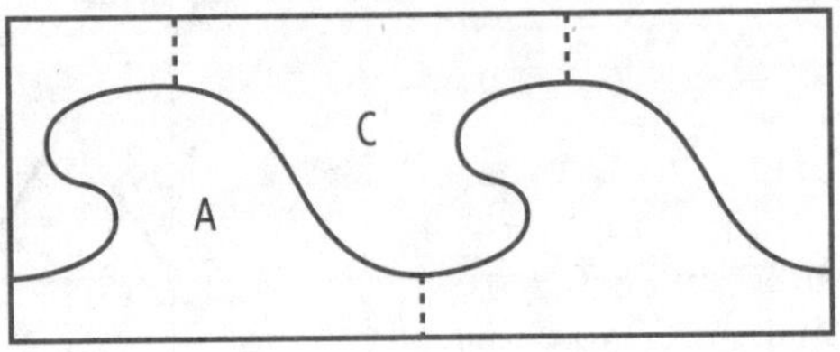

HABITS OF MIND

Model With Mathematics How can you determine whether two real-world figures are congruent?

Do You UNDERSTAND?

1. ESSENTIAL QUESTION What is the relationship between rigid motions and congruence?

2. **Error Analysis** Taylor says *ABCD* and *EFGH* are congruent because he can map *ABCD* to *EFGH* by multiplying each side length by 1.5 and translating the result to coincide with *EFGH*. What is Taylor's error?

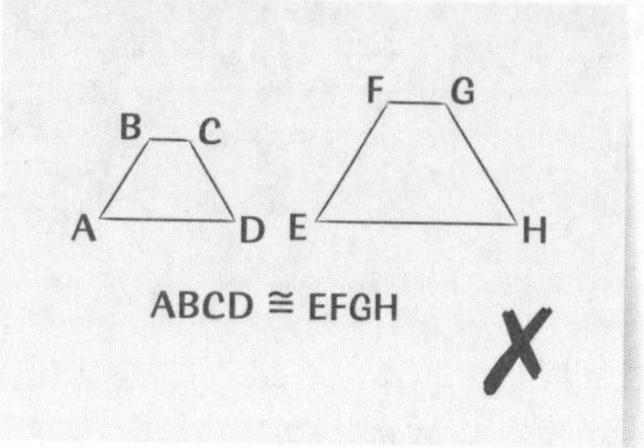

3. **Vocabulary** Why is a rigid motion also called a congruence transformation?

4. **Reason** For any two line segments that are congruent, what must be true about the lengths of the segments?

5. **Construct Arguments** A composition of rigid motions maps one figure to another figure. Is each intermediate image in the composition congruent to the original and final figures? Explain.

6. **Communicate Precisely** Describe how you can find a rigid motion or composition of rigid motions to map a segment to a congruent segment and an angle to a congruent angle.

Do You KNOW HOW?

7. Given $ABCD \cong EFGH$, what rigid motion, or composition of rigid motions maps *ABCD* to *EFGH*?

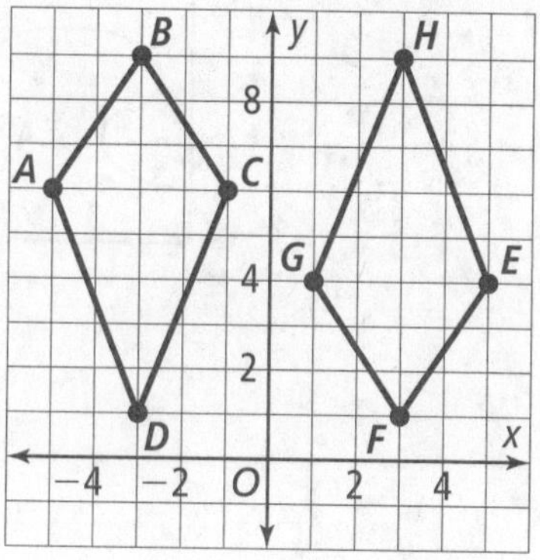

8. Which triangles are congruent?

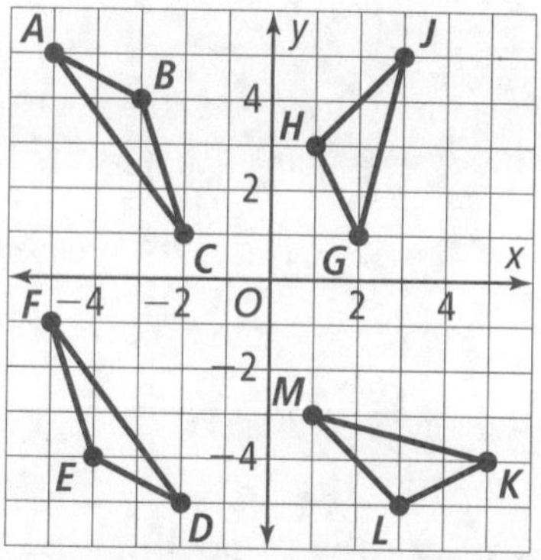

9. Are Figure A and Figure B congruent? If so, describe a composition of rigid motions that maps Figure A to Figure B. If not, explain.

Figure A Figure B

Activity

9-2 Isosceles and Equilateral Triangles

SavvasRealize.com

EXPLORE & REASON

Cut out a triangle with two sides of equal length from a piece of paper and label its angles 1, 2, and 3. Trace the outline of your triangle on another sheet of paper and label the angles.

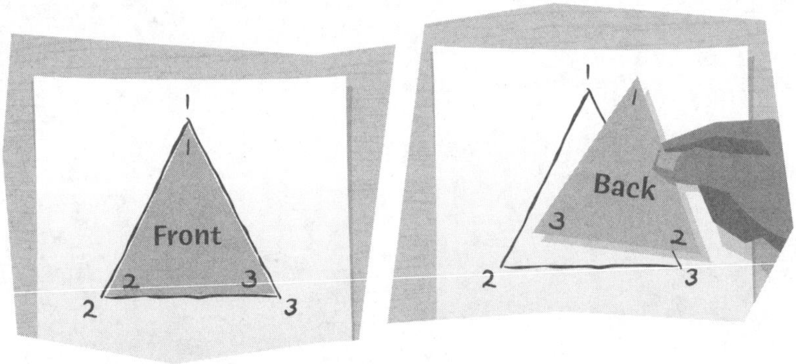

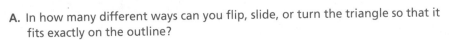

A. In how many different ways can you flip, slide, or turn the triangle so that it fits exactly on the outline?

B. Look for Relationships How do the angles and sides of the outline correspond to the angles and sides of the triangle?

C. How would your answer to Part A change if all three sides of the triangle were of equal length?

HABITS OF MIND

Generalize Will this process work with any other triangles? Explain.

EXAMPLE 1

Try It! Understand Angles of Isosceles Triangles

1. Copy isosceles $\triangle ABC$. Reflect the triangle across line BC to create the image $\triangle C'B'A'$. What rigid motion maps $\triangle C'B'A'$ onto $\triangle ABC$? Can you use this to show that $\angle A \cong \angle C$? Explain.

EXAMPLE 2

Try It! Use the Isosceles Triangle Theorem

2. What is the value of x?

a.

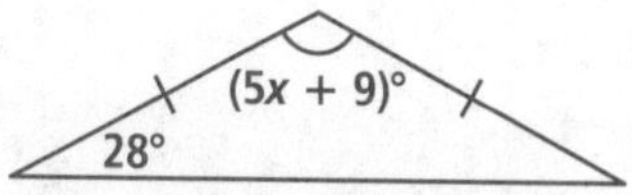

b.

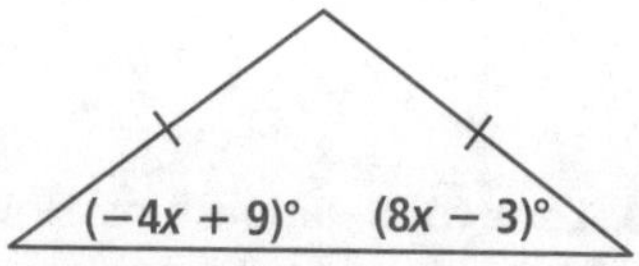

HABITS OF MIND

Communicate Precisely Given the angle measure of the vertex angle, how can you find the measures of the base angles?

Notes

EXAMPLE 3

Try It! Use the Converse of the Isosceles Triangle Theorem

3. Use the figure shown.

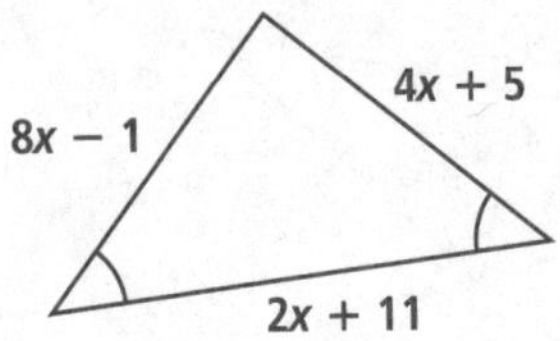

a. What is the value of x?

b. What are the lengths of all three sides of the triangle?

Notes

EXAMPLE 4

Try It! Use Perpendicular Bisectors to Solve Problems

4. Use the figure shown.

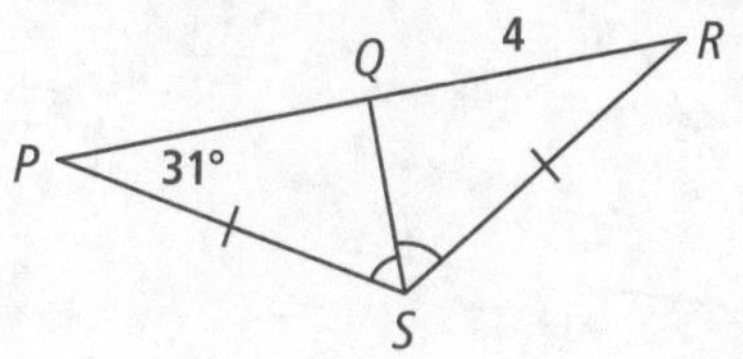

a. What is $m\angle RSQ$?

b. What is PR?

HABITS OF MIND

Generalize How do you know that any isosceles triangle can be decomposed into two congruent right triangles?

Assess

EXAMPLE 5

Try It! Prove that Equilateral Triangles are Equiangular

5. What rotation can be used to show the angles of an equilateral triangle are congruent?

EXAMPLE 6

Try It! Find Angle Measures in Isosceles and Equilateral Triangles

6. Find each angle measure in the figure.

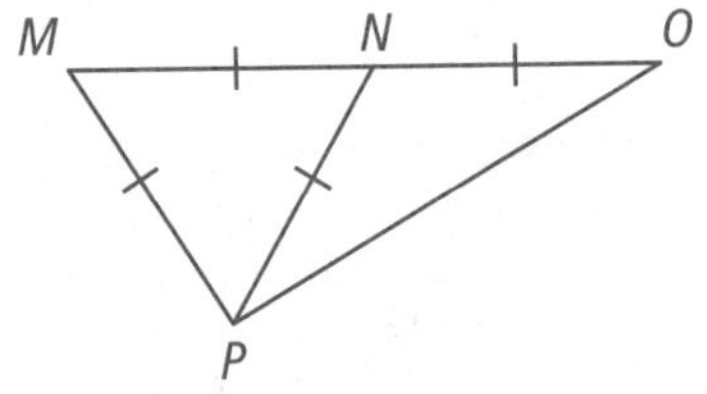

a. $m\angle PNO$

b. $m\angle NOP$

HABITS OF MIND

Reason How do you know what the measures of the angles of an equilateral triangle are?

Do You UNDERSTAND?

1. ESSENTIAL QUESTION How are the side lengths and angle measures related in isosceles triangles and in equilateral triangles?

2. **Error Analysis** Nate drew the following diagram to represent an equilateral triangle and an isosceles triangle. What mistake did Nate make?

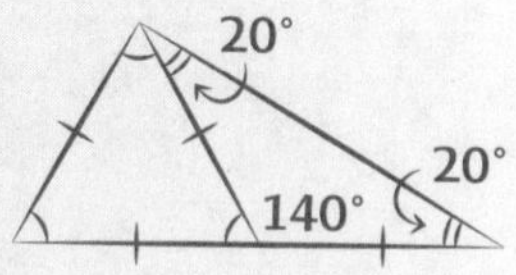

3. **Vocabulary** How can you distinguish the base of an isosceles triangle from a leg?

4. **Reason** Is it possible for the vertex of an isosceles triangle to be a right angle? Explain why or why not, and state the angle measures of the triangle, if possible.

5. **Communicate Precisely** Describe five rigid motions that map equilateral triangle $\triangle PQR$ onto itself.

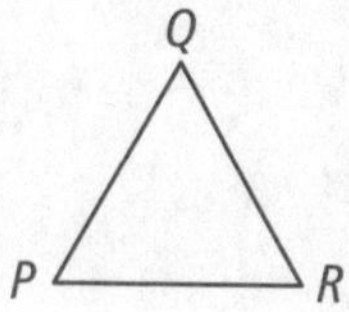

Do You KNOW HOW?

For Exercises 6 and 7, find the unknown angle measures.

6.

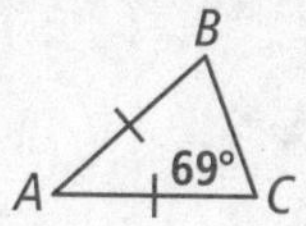

7.

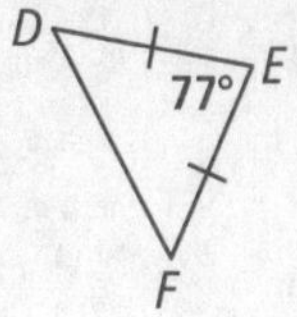

For Exercises 8 and 9, find the lengths of all three sides of the triangle.

8.

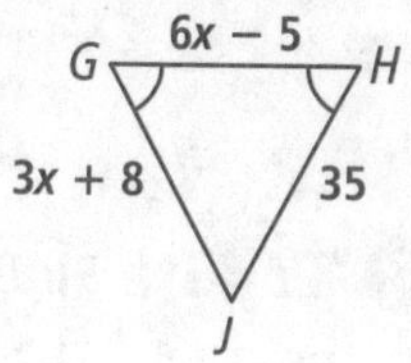

9.

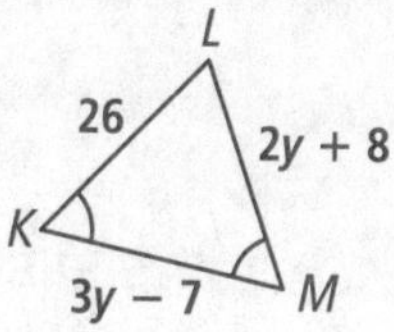

10. What is $m\angle ABD$ in the figure?

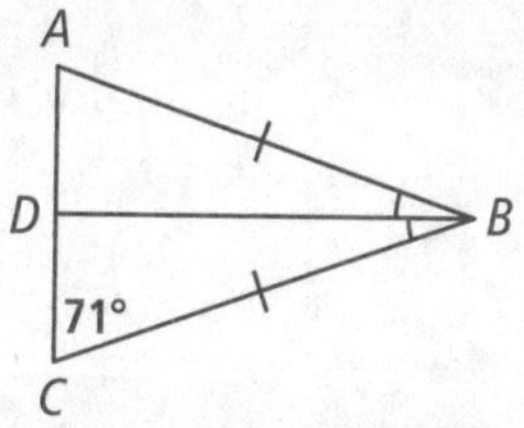

11. A light is suspended between two poles as shown. How far above the ground is the light? Round to the nearest tenth of a foot.

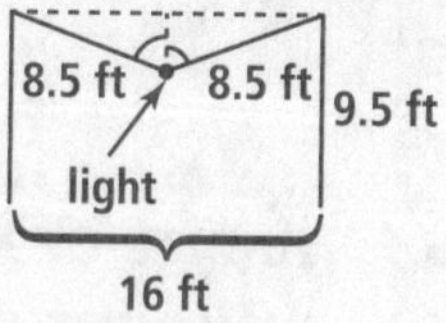

Video

MATHEMATICAL MODELING IN 3 ACTS

SavvasRealize.com

Check It Out!

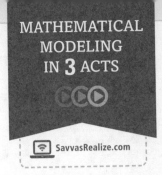

Maybe you've played this game before: you draw a picture. Then you try to get a classmate to draw the same picture by giving step-by-step directions but without showing your drawings.

Try it with a classmate. Draw a map of a room in your house or a place in your town. Then give directions to a classmate to draw the map that you drew. How similar are they? Think about this during the Mathematical Modeling in 3 Acts lesson.

ACT 1 Identify the Problem

1. What is the first question that comes to mind after watching the video?

2. Write down the Main Question you will answer.

3. Make an initial conjecture that answers this Main Question.

4. Explain how you arrived at your conjecture.

5. What information will be useful to know to answer the main question? How can you get it? How will you use that information?

Video

ACT 2 Develop a Model

6. Use the math that you have learned in the topic to refine your conjecture.

ACT 3 Interpret the Results

7. Did your refined conjecture match the actual answer exactly? If not, what might explain the difference?

Activity

9-3 Proving and Applying the SAS and SSS Congruence Criteria

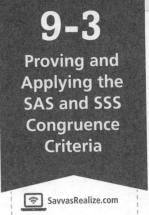

SavvasRealize.com

EXPLORE & REASON

Make five triangles that have a 5-inch side, a 6-inch side, and one 40° angle.

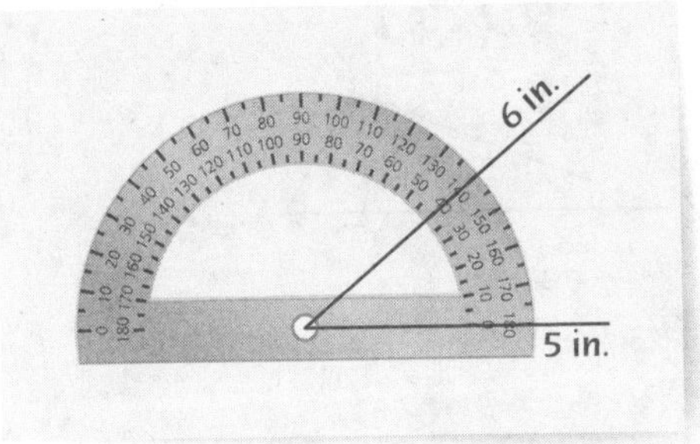

A. How many unique triangles can you make?

B. Construct Arguments How are the unique triangles different from each other?

HABITS OF MIND

Make Sense and Persevere How could you organize your work to make sure you have tried every possible combination of the given side lengths and angle measure?

Assess

EXAMPLE 1

Try It! Explore the Side-Angle-Side (SAS) Congruence Criterion

1. What rigid motion or composition of rigid motions shows that $\triangle UVW$ maps to $\triangle XYZ$?

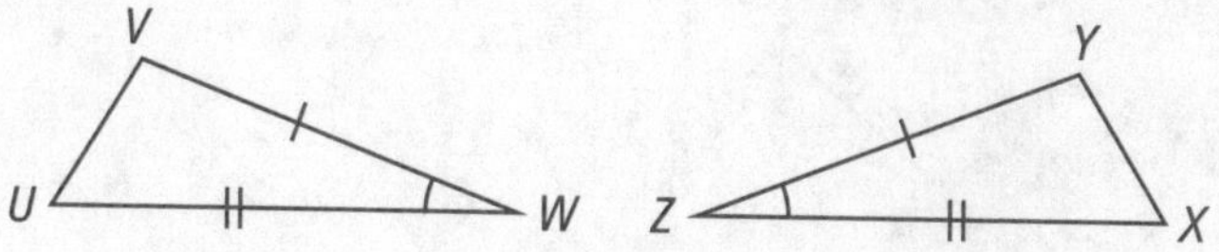

EXAMPLE 2

Try It! Apply the SAS Congruence Criterion

2. Given that $\overline{AB} \parallel \overline{CD}$ and $\overline{AB} \cong \overline{CD}$, how can you show that $\angle B \cong \angle D$?

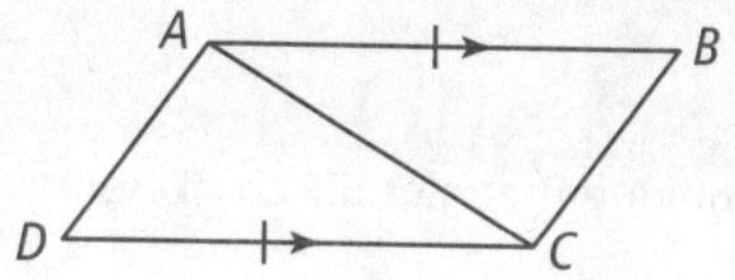

HABITS OF MIND

Reason How can knowing lines are parallel help establish triangle congruence by SAS?

EXAMPLE 3 **Try It!** **Prove the Side-Side-Side (SSS) Congruence Criterion**

3. Show that there is a rigid motion that maps △*PQR* to △*STU*.
Hint: Be sure to consider a reflection when mapping △*PQR* to △*STU*.

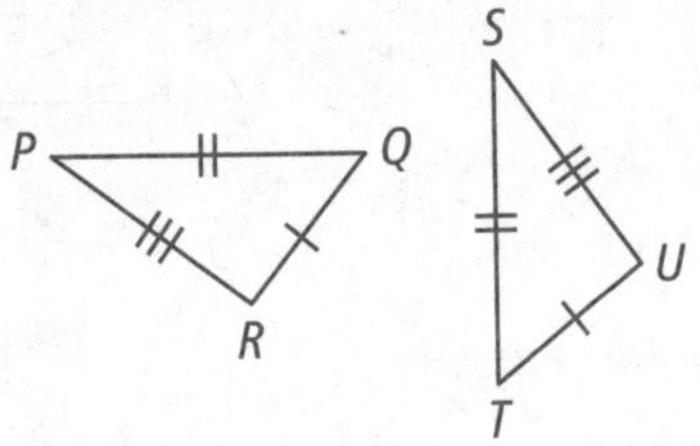

EXAMPLE 4 **Try It!** **Determine Congruent Triangles**

4. a. Is △*STU* congruent to △*XYZ*? Explain.

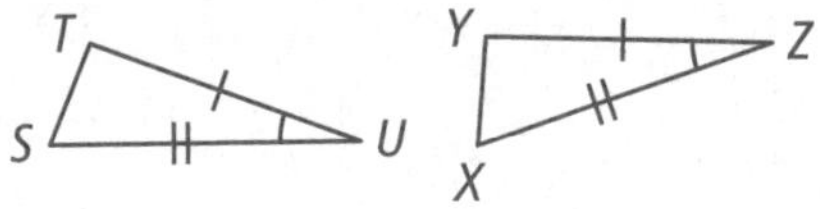

b. Is any additional information needed to show △*DEF* ≅ △*GHJ* by SAS? Explain.

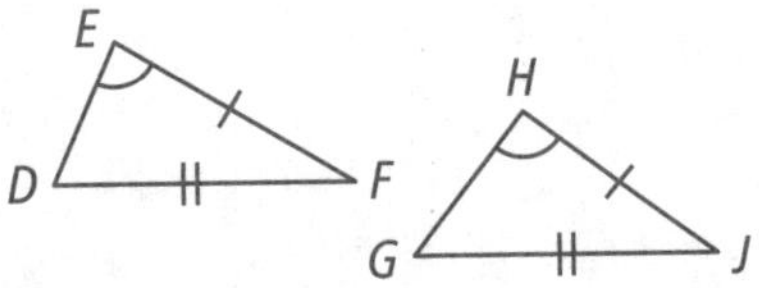

HABITS OF MIND

Look for Relationships How can you decide whether to choose either SAS or SSS to prove triangle congruence?

Do You UNDERSTAND?

1. **ESSENTIAL QUESTION** How are SAS and SSS used to show that two triangles are congruent?

2. **Error Analysis** Elijah says $\triangle ABC$ and $\triangle DEF$ are congruent by SAS. Explain Elijah's error.

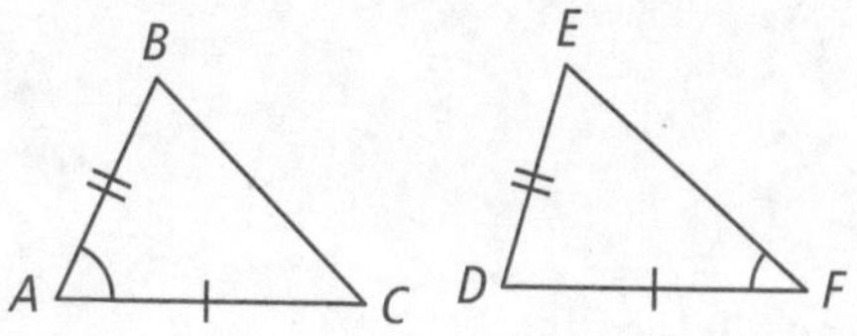

3. **Construct Arguments** Suppose $\overline{PR} \cong \overline{ST}$ and $\angle P \cong \angle S$. Ron wants prove $\triangle PQR \cong \triangle STU$ by SAS. He says all he needs to do is to show $\overline{RQ} \cong \overline{SU}$. Will that work? Explain.

4. **Reason** How would you decide what theorem to use to prove $\angle JKL \cong \angle MNP$? Explain.

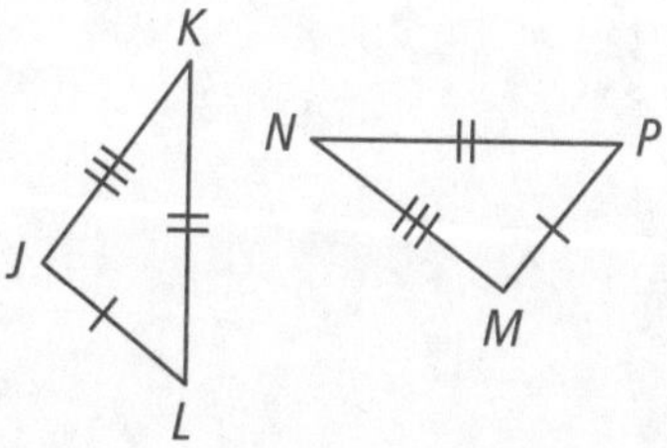

5. **Make Sense and Persevere** Suppose that $\overline{JK}$ and $\overline{LM}$ bisect each other. Is there enough information to show that $\triangle JPM \cong \triangle KPL$? Explain.

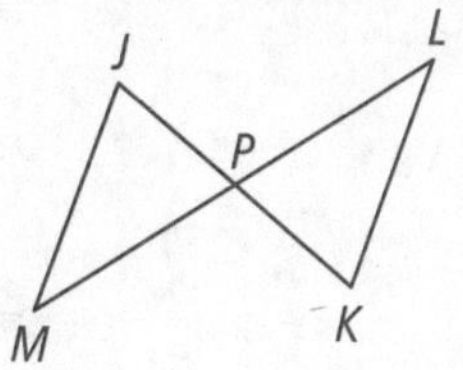

Do You KNOW HOW?

For Exercises 6–8, which pairs of triangles are congruent by SAS? By SSS?

6.

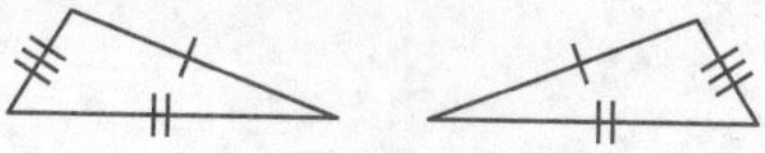

7.

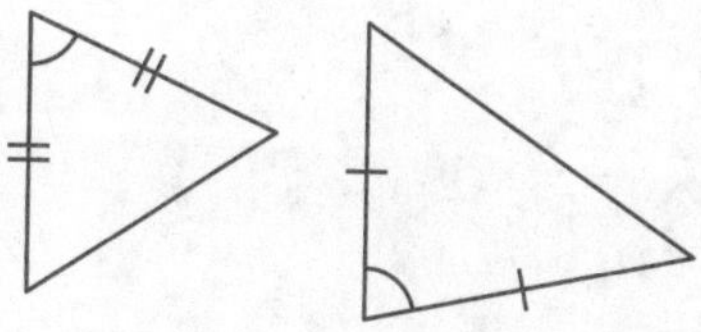

8.

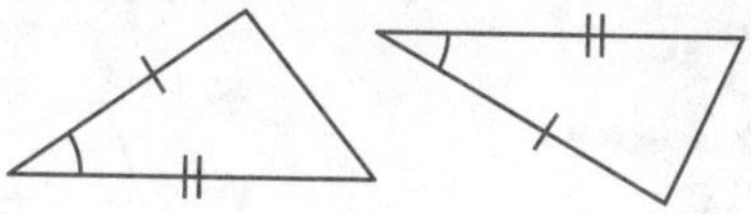

For Exercises 9–11, are the triangles congruent? Explain.

9.

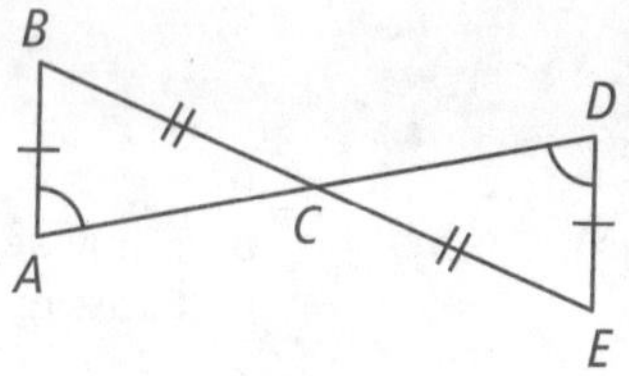

10.

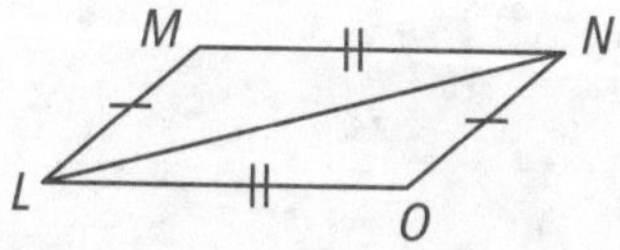

11.

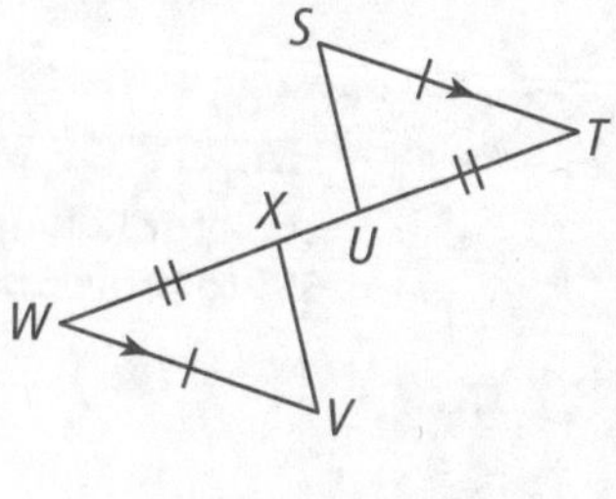

Activity

9-4 Proving and Applying the ASA and AAS Congruence Criteria

SavvasRealize.com

EXPLORE & REASON

Are these triangles congruent?

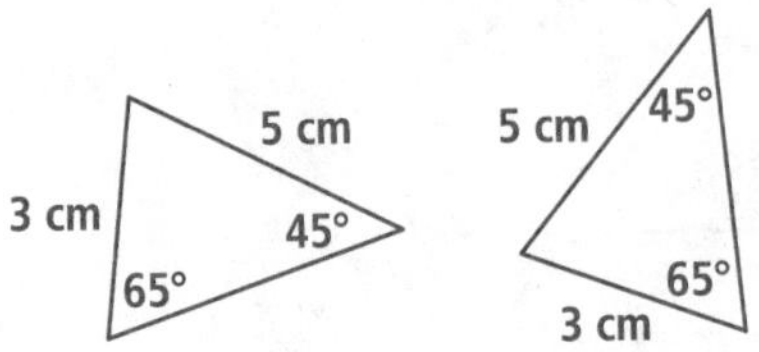

A. Make Sense and Persevere Assume the triangles are *not* congruent. What contradictions can you find to contradict your assumption? Explain.

B. Is it sufficient to say that the triangles are congruent because of the contradictions you found? Explain.

HABITS OF MIND

Generalize Is there a mathematical rule for proving that these triangles are congruent?

Notes

Assess

EXAMPLE 1

Try It! Explore the Angle-Side-Angle (ASA) Congruence Criterion

1. What is the relationship between $\triangle AXB$ and $\triangle AYB$?

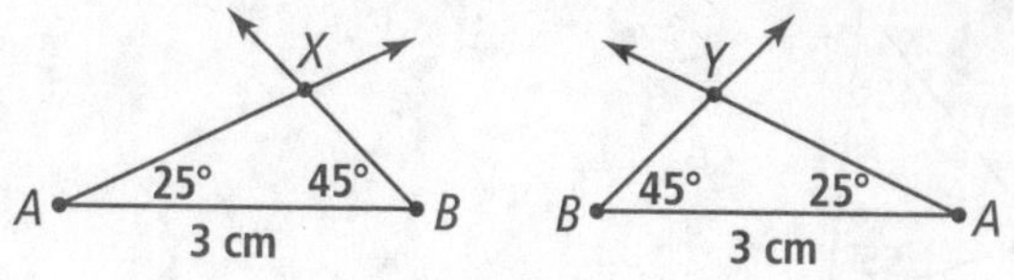

EXAMPLE 2

Try It! Prove the Angle-Side-Angle (ASA) Congruence Criterion

2. Describe a series of transformations that shows $\triangle JKL \cong \triangle MNO$.

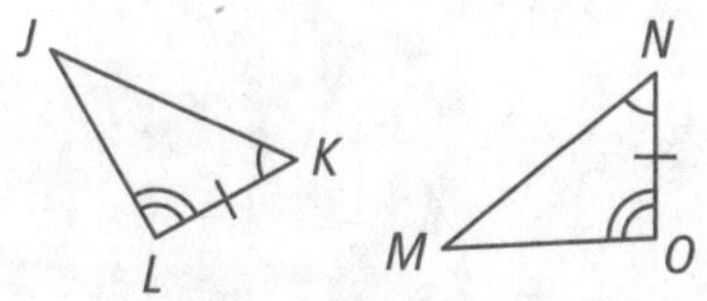

EXAMPLE 3

Try It! Apply the Angle-Side-Angle (ASA) Congruence Criterion

3. Use the figures shown.

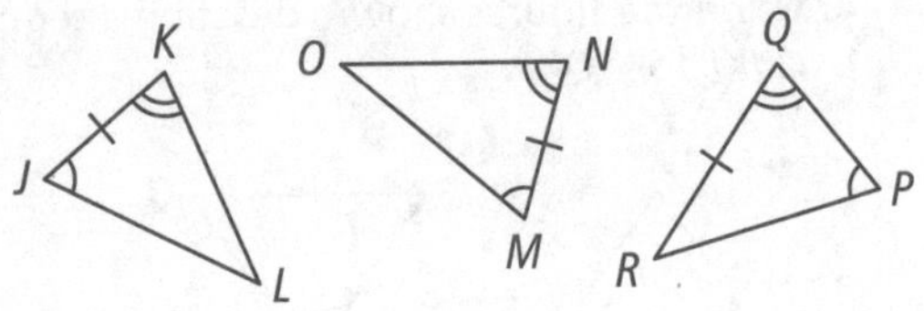

a. Are $\triangle JKL$ and $\triangle MNO$ congruent? Explain.

b. Are $\triangle JKL$ and $\triangle PQR$ congruent? Explain.

HABITS OF MIND

Communicate Precisely What properties can you use to show that angles are congruent?

EXAMPLE 4

Try It! Investigate the Angle-Angle-Side (AAS) Congruence Criterion

4. Using the figures shown, describe a sequence of rigid motions that maps $\triangle JKL$ to $\triangle QRP$.

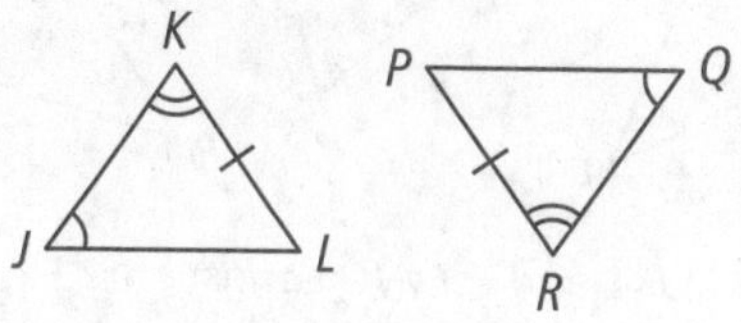

EXAMPLE 5

Try It! Use Triangle Congruence Criteria

5. Use the figures shown.

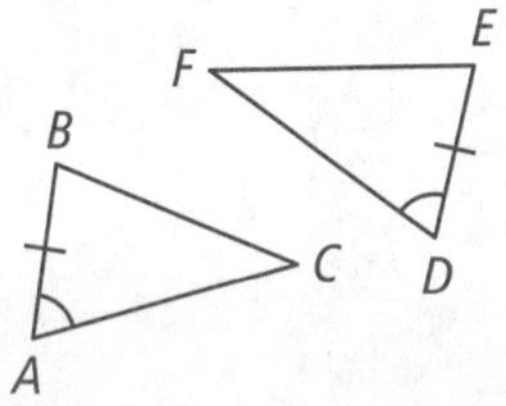

a. What additional information is needed to show $\triangle ABC \cong \triangle DEF$ by ASA?

b. What additional information is needed to show $\triangle ABC \cong \triangle DEF$ by AAS?

HABITS OF MIND

Construct Arguments How can it be helpful to assume the opposite of what you have been asked to prove?

EXAMPLE 6

Try It! Determine Congruent Polygons

6. Given $ABCD \cong EFGH$, what is the value of x?

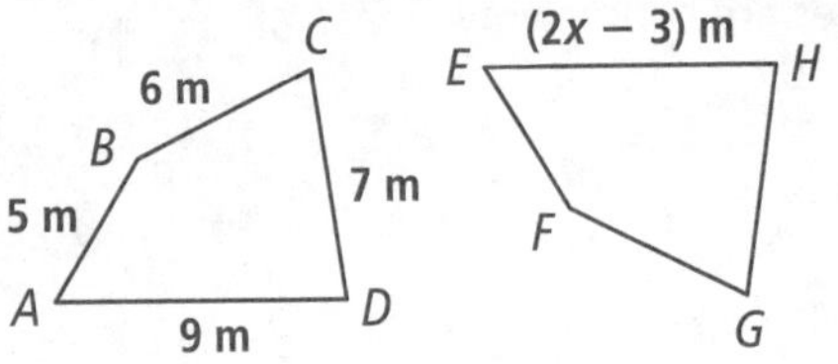

HABITS OF MIND

Generalize How does identifying congruent triangles help you show that polygons are congruent?

Do You UNDERSTAND?

1. **ESSENTIAL QUESTION** How are ASA and AAS used to show that triangles are congruent?

2. **Error Analysis** Why is Terrell's conclusion incorrect?

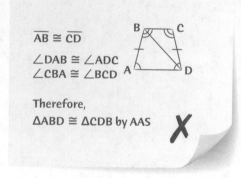

$\overline{AB} \cong \overline{CD}$

$\angle DAB \cong \angle ADC$
$\angle CBA \cong \angle BCD$

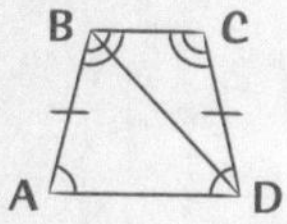

Therefore,
$\triangle ABD \cong \triangle CDB$ by AAS ✗

3. **Reason** How can you tell which property of triangle congruence shows $\triangle RST \cong \triangle UVW$?

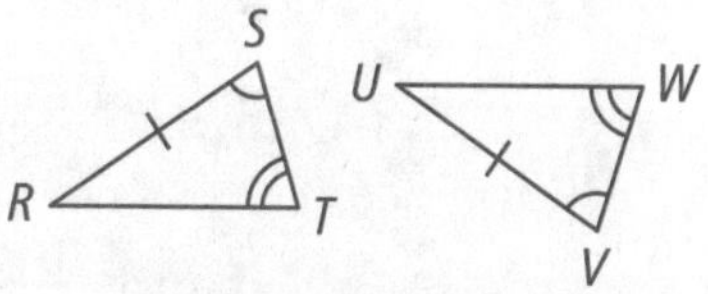

4. **Make Sense and Persevere** Is there a congruence relationship that is sufficient to show that $\triangle MNO \cong \triangle TUV$? Explain.

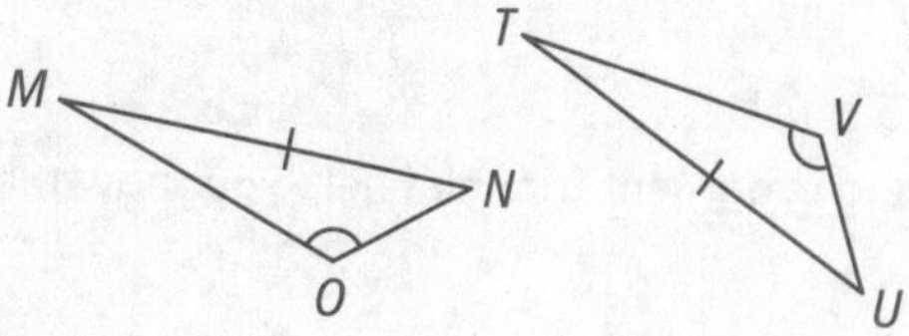

Do You KNOW HOW?

For Exercises 5 and 6, find the value of *x*.

5.

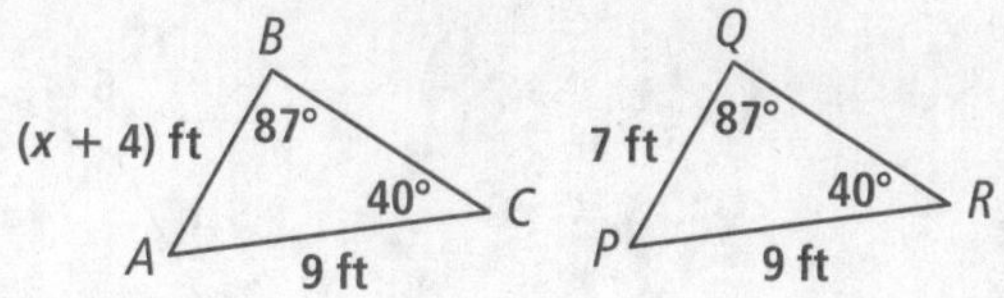

6.

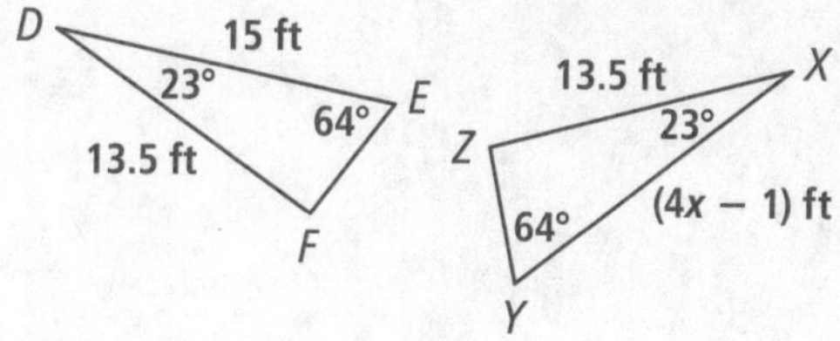

For Exercises 7 and 8, state whether the triangles are congruent and by which theorem.

7.

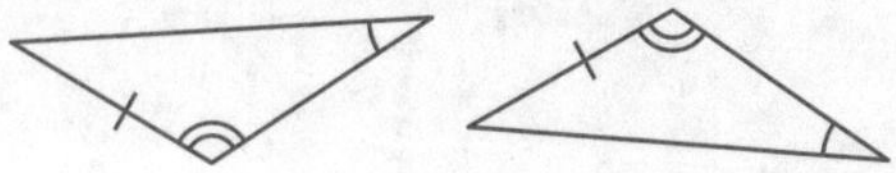

8.

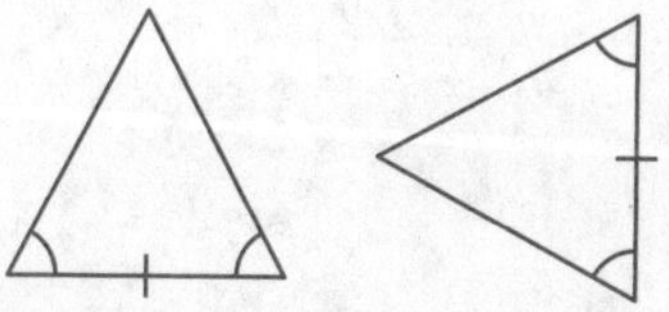

9. Why is $LMNO \cong PQRS$?

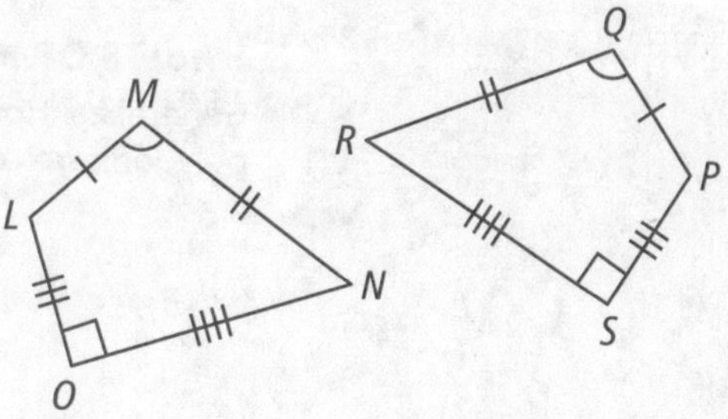

9-5 Congruence in Right Triangles

CRITIQUE & EXPLAIN

Seth and Jae wrote the following explanations of why the two triangles are congruent.

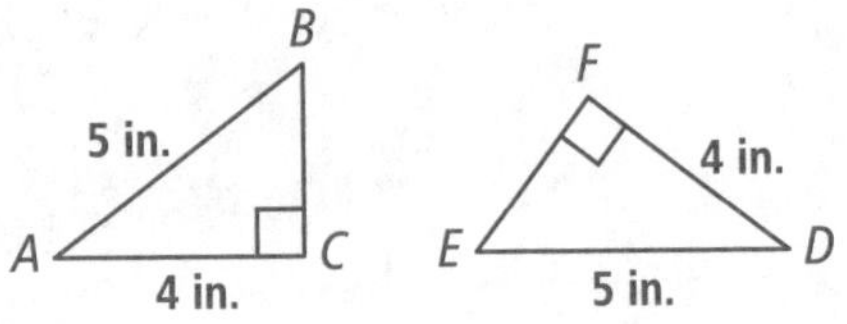

Seth

There are two pairs of congruent sides, $\overline{AB} \cong \overline{DE}$ and $\overline{AC} \cong \overline{DF}$, and a pair of congruent right angles, $\angle C \cong \angle F$. So $\triangle ABC \cong \triangle DEF$ by SSA.

Jae

The lengths of $\overline{BC}$ and $\overline{EF}$ are 3 in., since these are 3-4-5 right triangles. There are three pairs of congruent sides, $\overline{AB} \cong \overline{DE}$, $\overline{AC} \cong \overline{DF}$, and $\overline{BC} \cong \overline{EF}$. So $\triangle ABC \cong \triangle DEF$ by SSS.

A. Do you think either student is correct? Explain.

B. **Communicate Precisely** Describe when you can state that two right triangles are congruent if you are only given two pairs of congruent sides and a right angle in each triangle.

HABITS OF MIND

Make Sense and Persevere Could you use Jae's strategy if the dimensions of the triangles were different?

EXAMPLE 1

Try It! Investigate Right Triangle Congruence

1. Can you show that two right triangles are congruent when any one pair of corresponding acute angles is congruent and any one pair of corresponding legs is congruent? Explain.

EXAMPLE 2

Try It! Use the Hypotenuse-Leg (HL) Theorem

2. What information is needed in order to apply the Hypotenuse-Leg (HL) Theorem?

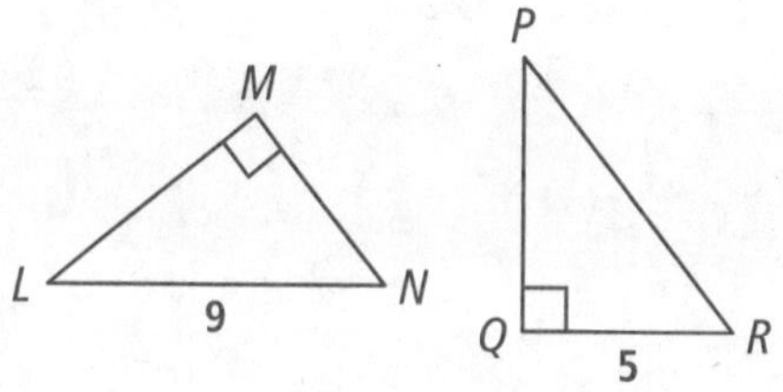

HABITS OF MIND

Look for Relationships What are the relationships that you could use to show that two right triangles are congruent?

Assess

EXAMPLE 3 Try It! Write a Proof Using the Hypotenuse-Leg (HL) Theorem

3. Write a proof to show that two triangles are congruent.

Given: $\overline{JL} \perp \overline{KM}$, $\overline{JK} \cong \overline{LK}$

Prove: $\triangle JKM \cong \triangle LKM$

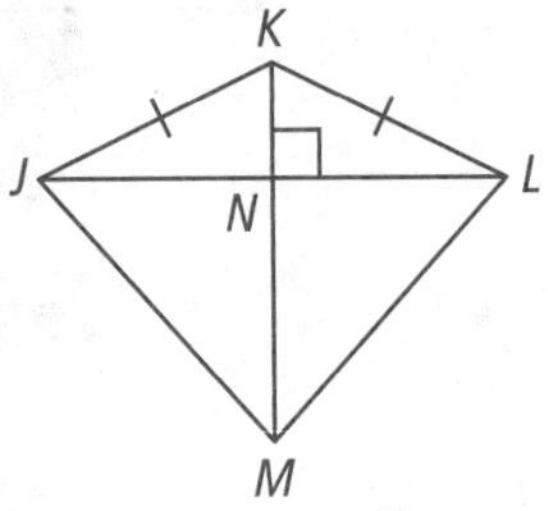

HABITS OF MIND

Make Sense and Persevere What observations do you need to make to write a proof showing that two triangles are congruent?

Do You UNDERSTAND?

1. ESSENTIAL QUESTION What minimum criteria are needed to show that right triangles are congruent?

2. **Error Analysis** Yama stated that $\triangle KLM \cong \triangle PLN$ by the HL Theorem. What mistake did Yama make?

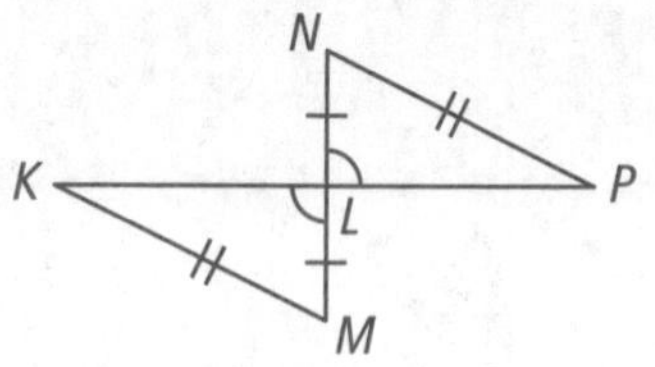

3. **Use Structure** What are the three conditions that two triangles must meet in order to apply the HL Theorem?

4. **Reason** The HL Theorem is a side-side-angle theorem for right triangles. Why does it prove congruence for two right triangles but not prove congruence for two acute triangles or for two obtuse triangles?

Do You KNOW HOW?

What information is needed to prove the triangles are congruent using the Hypotenuse-Leg (HL) Theorem?

5.

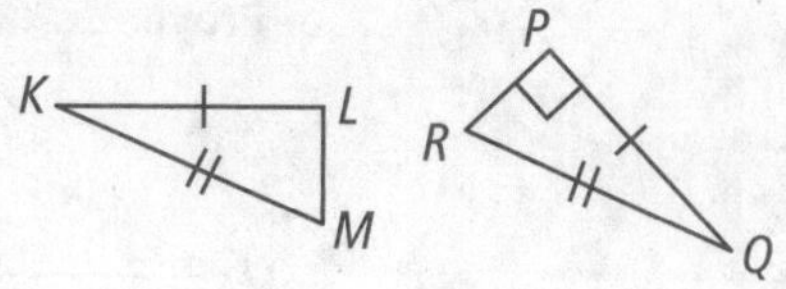

6.

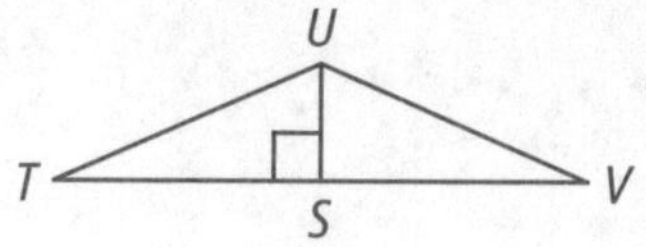

What information would be sufficient to show the two triangles are congruent by the Hypotenuse-Leg (HL) Theorem?

7.

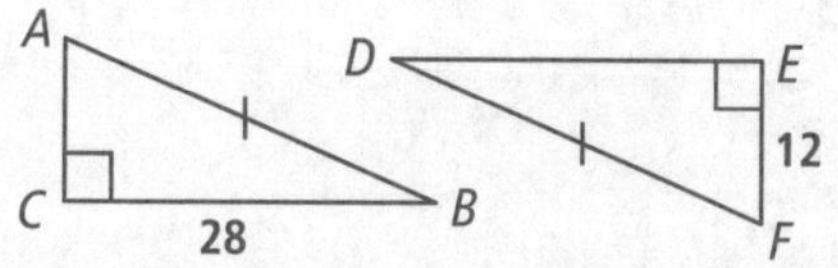

8.

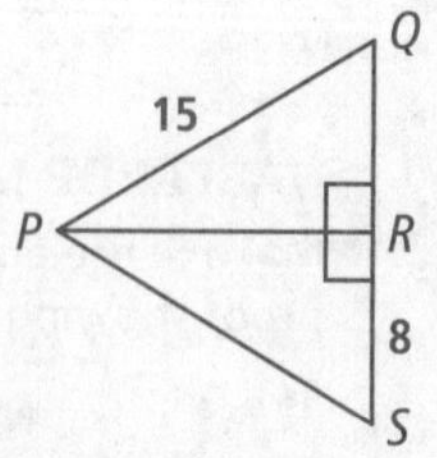

9-6 Congruence in Overlapping Triangles

SavvasRealize.com

EXPLORE & REASON

Look at the painting shown.

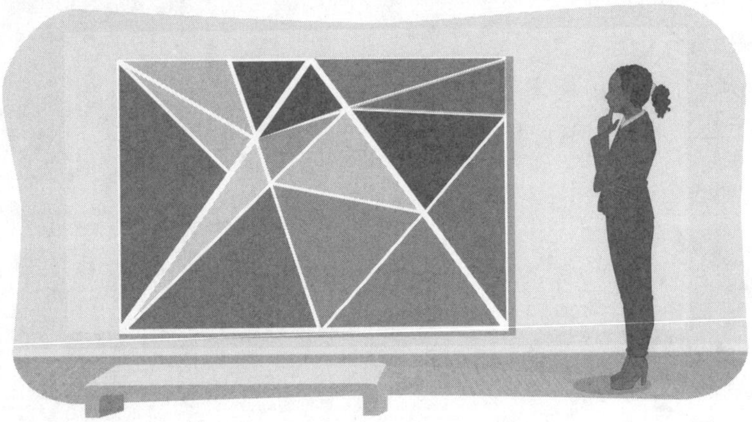

A. How many triangles can you find?

B. Make Sense and Persevere What strategy did you use to count the triangles? How well did your strategy work?

HABITS OF MIND

Make Sense and Persevere What are some other strategies you might try to help you find all the triangles?

✎ Notes

Assess

EXAMPLE 1

Try It! Identify Corresponding Parts in Triangles

1. What are the corresponding sides and angles in $\triangle FHJ$ and $\triangle KHG$?

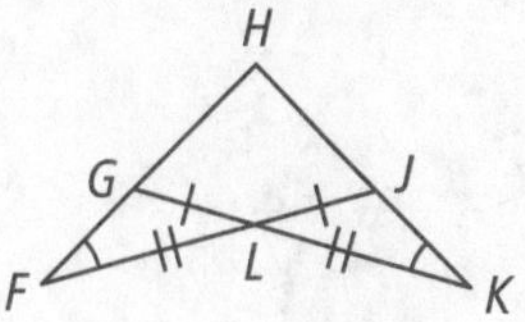

EXAMPLE 2

Try It! Use Common Parts of Triangles

2. Are $\overline{VW}$ and $\overline{ZY}$ congruent? Explain.

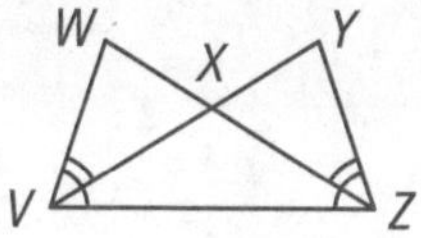

HABITS OF MIND

Generalize Could there be more than one correct way to assign corresponding vertices in two congruent triangles? Explain.

Assess

EXAMPLE 3

Try It! Prove That Two Triangles Are Congruent

3. Write a proof to show that $\triangle SRV \cong \triangle TUW$.

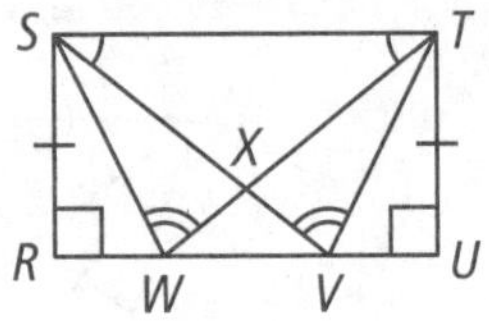

EXAMPLE 4

Try It! Separate Overlapping Triangles

4. A new route will stop at the History Museum, Water Park, Zoo, Science Museum, and Theater. Draw a triangle to represent the new route. Include any length or angle information that is given in the diagram.

HABITS OF MIND

Look for Relationships What are some observations about the different ways triangles can overlap?

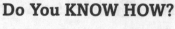

Do You UNDERSTAND?

1. ESSENTIAL QUESTION Which theorems can be used to prove two overlapping triangles are congruent?

2. Construct Arguments How could you prove that $\triangle ACD \cong \triangle ECB$?

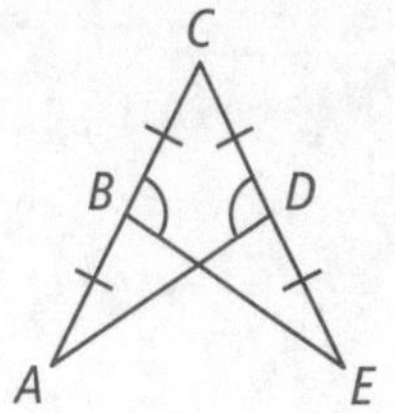

3. Error Analysis Nicholas wrote a proof to show that $\triangle EFD \cong \triangle DGE$. Explain Nicholas's error. Is it possible to prove the triangles congruent? Explain.

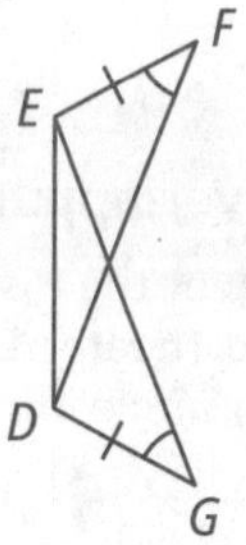

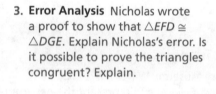

Since $\overline{EF} \cong \overline{DG}$, $\angle F \cong \angle G$, and $\overline{ED} \cong \overline{ED}$, by SAS, $\Delta EFD \cong \Delta DGE$. ✗

4. Use Structure Quadrilateral *JKLM* is a rectangle. Which triangles are congruent to $\triangle JKL$? Explain.

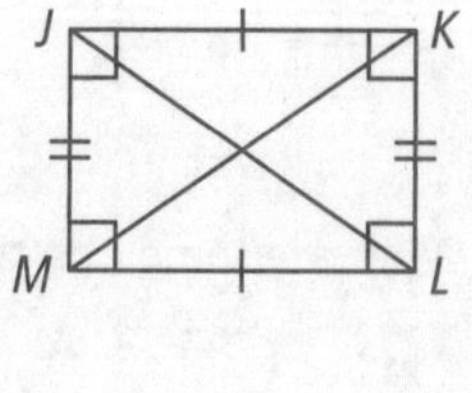

Do You KNOW HOW?

5. What are the corresponding sides and angles in $\triangle WXV$ and $\triangle XWY$?

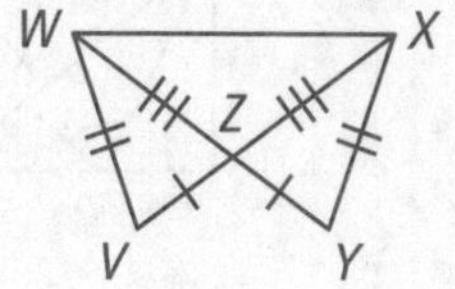

In Exercises 6–9, name a side or angle congruent to each given side or angle.

6. $\angle CDA$

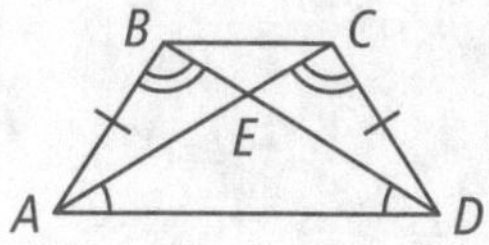

7. $\overline{DB}$

8. $\angle FGH$

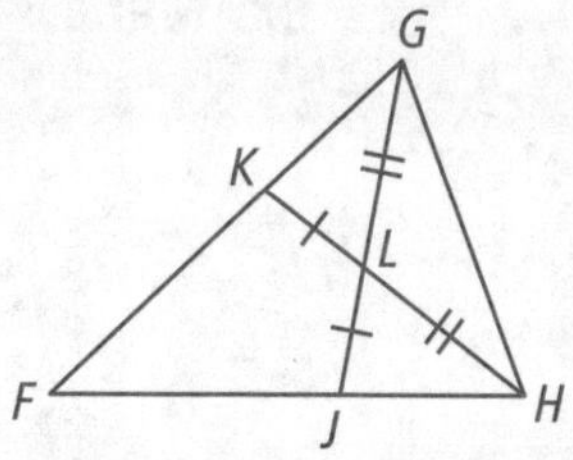

9. $\overline{HJ}$

For Exercises 10 and 11, name a theorem that can be used to prove that each pair of triangles is congruent.

10. $\triangle GJL$ and $\triangle KHL$

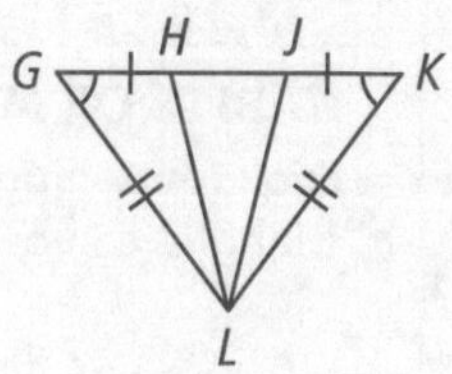

11. $\triangle NQM$ and $\triangle PMQ$

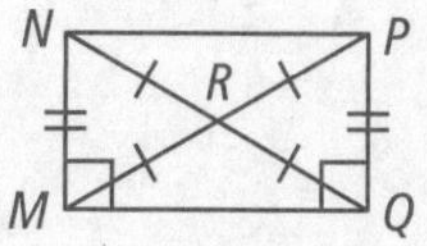

Activity

9-7 Polygons in the Coordinate Plane

SavvasRealize.com

EXPLORE & REASON

Players place game pieces on the board shown and earn points from the attributes of the piece placed on the board.

- 1 point for a right angle
- 2 points for a pair of parallel sides
- 3 points for the shortest perimeter

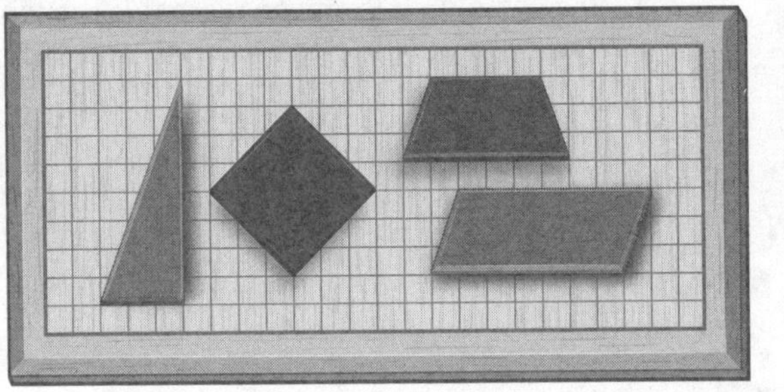

A. Which game piece is worth the greatest total points? Explain.

B. Make Sense and Persevere Describe a way to determine the perimeters that is different from the way you chose. Which method do you consider better? Explain.

HABITS OF MIND

Communicate Precisely How can you compare the lengths of sides of polygons that are placed on grids?

Notes

Assess

EXAMPLE 1

Try It! Connect Algebra and Geometry Through Coordinates

1. Given $\triangle ABC$ in Example 1, what is the length of the line segment connecting the midpoints of $\overline{AC}$ and $\overline{BC}$?

EXAMPLE 2

Try It! Classify a Triangle on the Coordinate Plane

2. The vertices of $\triangle PQR$ are $P(4, 1)$, $Q(2, 7)$, and $R(8, 5)$.

   a. Is $\triangle PQR$ equilateral, isosceles, or scalene? Explain.

   b. Is $\triangle PQR$ a right triangle? Explain.

HABITS OF MIND

Look for Relationships Given the vertices of a triangle on a coordinate plane, what formulas can you use to determine the type of triangle? Explain.

Notes

Assess

EXAMPLE 3

Try It! Classify a Parallelogram on the Coordinate Plane

3. The vertices of a parallelogram are $A(-2, 2)$, $B(4, 6)$, $C(6, 3)$, and $D(0, -1)$.

   a. Is *ABCD* a rhombus? Explain.

   b. Is *ABCD* a rectangle? Explain.

EXAMPLE 4

Try It! Classify Quadrilaterals as Trapezoids and Kites on a Coordinate Plane

4. Is each quadrilateral a kite, trapezoid, or neither?

   a.

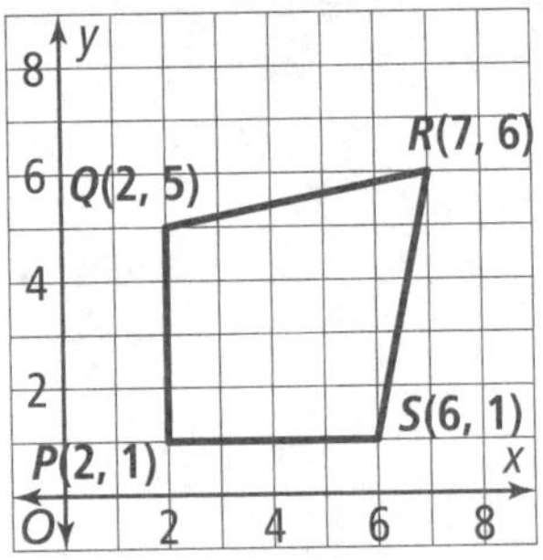

   b.

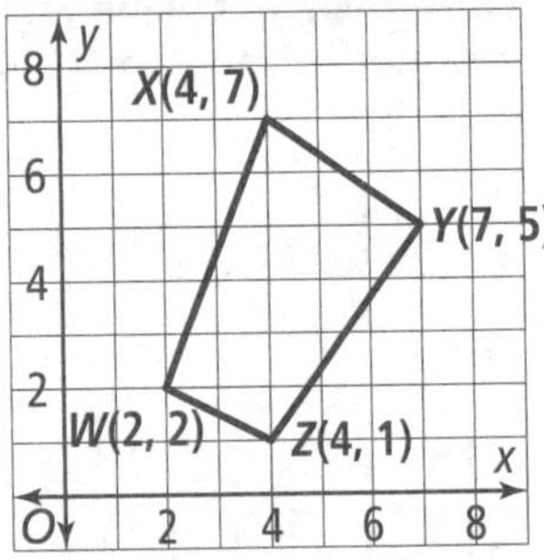

EXAMPLE 5

Try It! Find Perimeter and Area

5. The vertices of *WXYZ* are $W(5, 4)$, $X(2, 9)$, $Y(9, 9)$, and $Z(8, 4)$.

   a. What is the perimeter of *WXYZ*?

   b. What is the area of *WXYZ*?

HABITS OF MIND

Use Structure Can the slopes of three of the four sides of a quadrilateral be equal? Explain.

Assess

Do You UNDERSTAND?

1. **ESSENTIAL QUESTION** How are properties of geometric figures represented in the coordinate plane?

2. **Error Analysis** Chen is asked to describe two methods to find BC. Why is Chen incorrect?

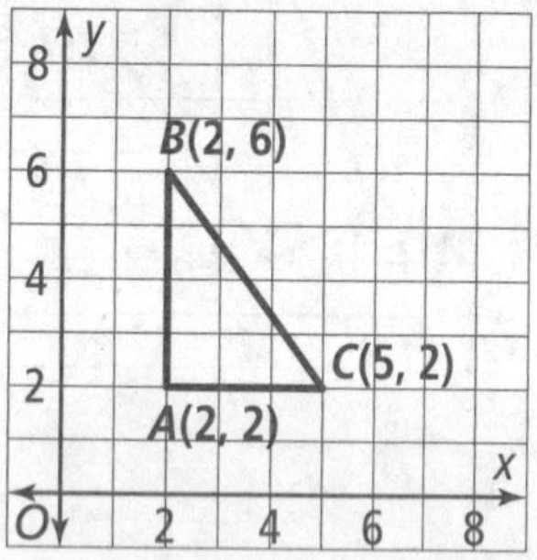

The only possible method is to use the Distance Formula because you only know the endpoints of $\overline{BC}$.

✗

3. **Communicate Precisely** Describe three ways you can determine whether a quadrilateral is a parallelogram given the coordinates of the vertices.

Do You KNOW HOW?

Use *JKLM* for Exercises 4–6.

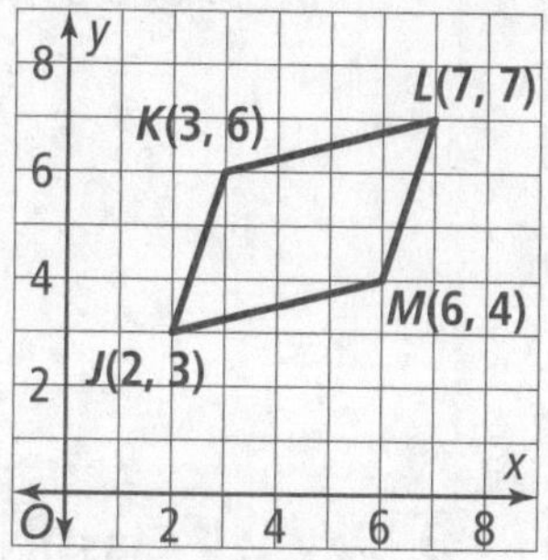

4. What is the perimeter of *JKLM*?

5. What is the relationship between $\overline{JL}$ and $\overline{KM}$? Explain.

6. What type of quadrilateral is *JKLM*? Explain.

Use $\triangle PQR$ for Exercises 7 and 8.

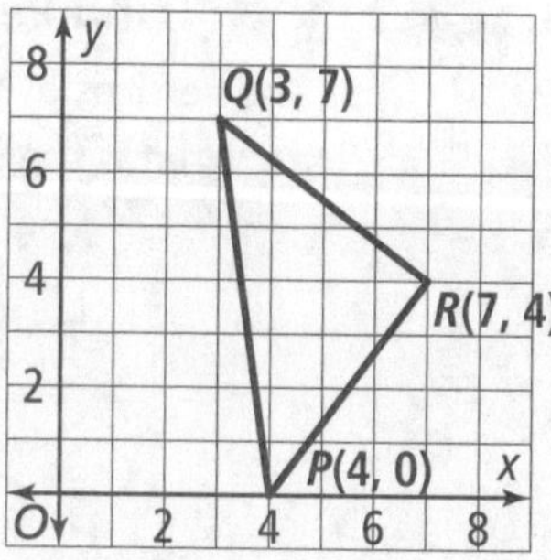

7. What kind of triangle is *PQR*? Explain.

8. What is the area of *PQR*?

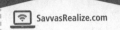

SavvasRealize.com

EXPLORE & REASON

Use the diagram to answer the questions.

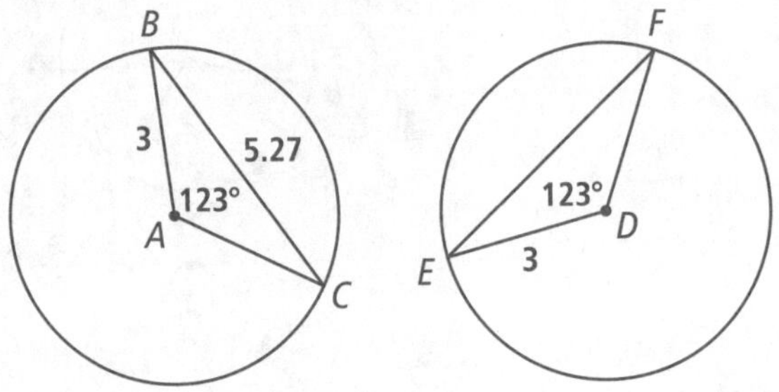

A. What figures in the diagram are congruent? Explain.

B. Look for Relationships How can you find *EF*?

HABITS OF MIND

Use Structure What is true of the radii of both circles? Explain.

Notes

Assess

EXAMPLE 1

Try It! Relate Central Angles and Chords

1. Why is $\angle BAC \cong \angle DAE$?

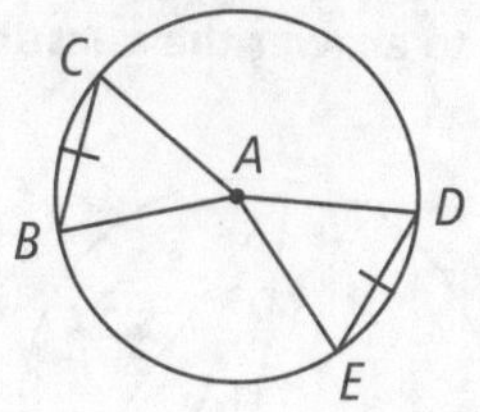

EXAMPLE 2

Try It! Relate Arcs and Chords

2. Write a flow proof of the Converse of Theorem 10-4.

EXAMPLE 3

Try It! Relate Chords Equidistant from the Center

3. Write a flow proof of the Converse of Theorem 10-5.

HABITS OF MIND

Generalize In the same circle or in congruent circles, what is true about congruent chords?

Assess

EXAMPLE 4

Try It! Construct a Regular Hexagon Inscribed in a Circle

4. Construct an equilateral triangle inscribed in a circle.

EXAMPLE 5

Try It! Solve Problems Involving Chords of Circles

5. Fresh cut flowers need to be in at least 4 inches of water. A spherical vase is filled until the surface of the water is a circle 5 inches in diameter. Is the water deep enough for the flowers? Explain.

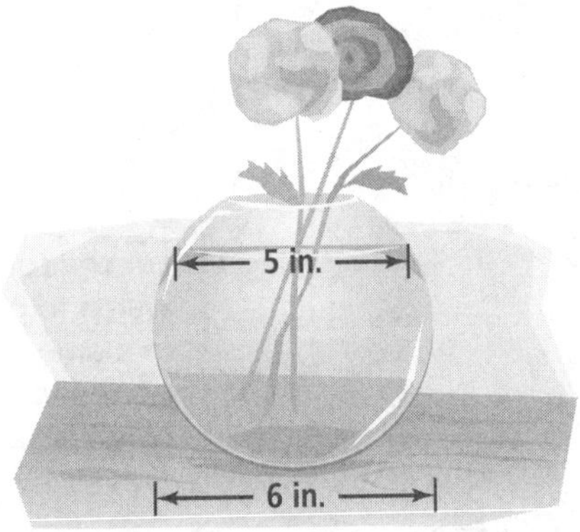

HABITS OF MIND

Reason What is the first thing to look for when solving problems involving chords and diameters?

Do You UNDERSTAND?

1. **ESSENTIAL QUESTION** How are chords related to their central angles and intercepted arcs?

2. **Error Analysis** Sasha writes a proof to show that two chords are congruent. What is her error?

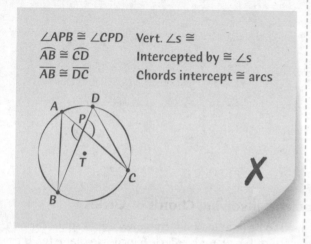

$\angle APB \cong \angle CPD$	Vert. $\angle$s $\cong$
$\widehat{AB} \cong \widehat{CD}$	Intercepted by $\cong$ $\angle$s
$\overline{AB} \cong \overline{DC}$	Chords intercept $\cong$ arcs

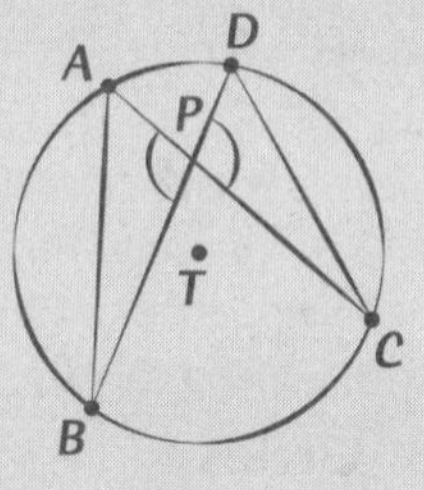

3. **Vocabulary** Explain why all diameters of circles are also chords of the circles.

4. **Reason** Given $\widehat{RS} \cong \widehat{UT}$, how can find UT?

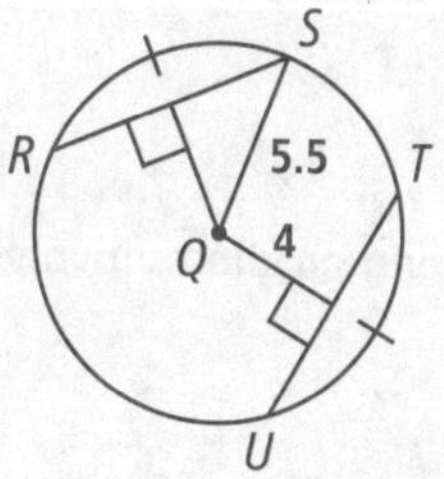

Do You KNOW HOW?

For Exercises 5–10, in ⊙*P*, $m\widehat{AB} = 43°$, and $AC = DF$. Find each measure.

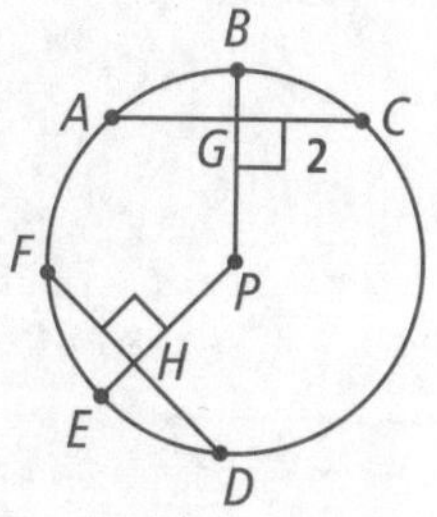

5. DF

6. $m\widehat{AC}$

7. FH

8. $m\widehat{DE}$

9. AC

10. $m\widehat{DF}$

11. For the corporate headquarters, an executive wants to place a company logo that is six feet in diameter with the sides of the H five feet tall on the front wall. What is the width x of the crossbar for the H?

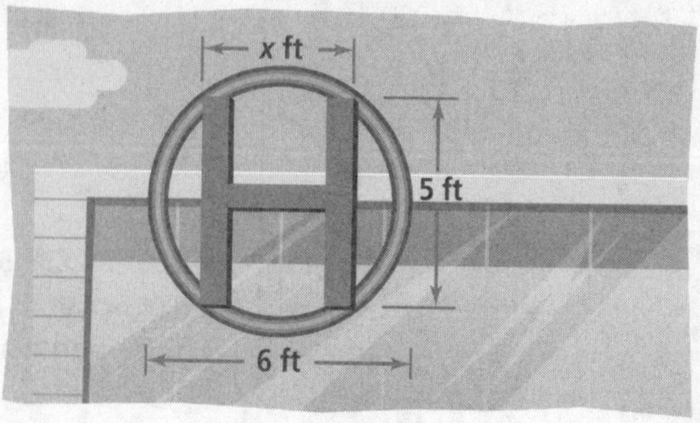

Activity

10-1 Analyzing Data Displays

SavvasRealize.com

MODEL & DISCUSS

MARKET RESEARCHERS WANTED!

A clothing company is designing a new line of shirts. Look around your classroom and collect data about the color of top worn by each student. If a student's top has multiple colors, choose the most prevalent one.

A. Explain why you chose to organize the data the way that you did.

B. How do you think the company could use these data?

C. **Use Appropriate Tools** How would you display these data in a presentation?

HABITS OF MIND

Reason What other information could you collect about the different types of shirts in your classroom? How could you organize these data?

Notes

Assess

EXAMPLE 1

Try It! Represent and Interpret Data in a Dot Plot

1. What might account for the outlier?

EXAMPLE 2

Try It! Represent and Interpret Data in a Histogram

2. What age group would be a good match for products advertised on this TV show? Explain.

HABITS OF MIND

Look for Relationships How is interpreting a histogram similar to interpreting a dot plot? How is it different?

EXAMPLE 3

Try It! Represent and Interpret Data in a Box Plot

3. Suppose Kaitlyn wants to make the statement that 25% of the students raised over a certain amount. What is that amount? Explain.

EXAMPLE 4

Try It! Choose a Data Display

4. Which data display should Helena use if she wants to know what percent of the teams scored higher than her team? Explain.

HABITS OF MIND

Use Appropriate Tools When is it useful to display data as a dot plot? When is it useful to display data as a histogram? When is it useful to display data as a box plot?

Assess

Do You UNDERSTAND?

1. ESSENTIAL QUESTION What information about data sets can you get from different data displays?

2. **Communicate Precisely** How is a dot plot different from a box plot? How are they similar?

3. **Use Appropriate Tools** If you want to see data values grouped in intervals, which data display should you choose? Explain.

4. **Error Analysis** Taylor says you can determine the mean of a data set from its box plot. Is Taylor correct? Explain your reasoning.

5. **Use Structure** Can you determine the minimum and maximum values of a data set simply by looking at its dot plot? Histogram? Box plot? Explain.

Do You KNOW HOW?

Use the data set shown for exercises 6–11.

7	5	8	15	4
9	10	1	12	8
13	7	11	8	10

6. Make a dot plot for the data. What information does the display reveal about the data set?

7. Make a histogram for the data. What information does the display reveal about the data set?

8. Make a box plot for the data. What information does the display reveal about the data set?

Identify the most appropriate data display to answer each question about the data set. Justify your response.

9. What is the median of the data set?

10. How many data values are greater than 7?

11. How many values fall in the interval 10 to 12?

CRITIQUE & EXPLAIN

The prices of paintings sold at two galleries in the last month are shown. Stacy and Diego both have a painting they want to sell.

- Stacy wants Gallery I to sell her painting because it has the highest sales price.
- Diego wants Gallery II to sell his painting because it has the most consistent sales prices.

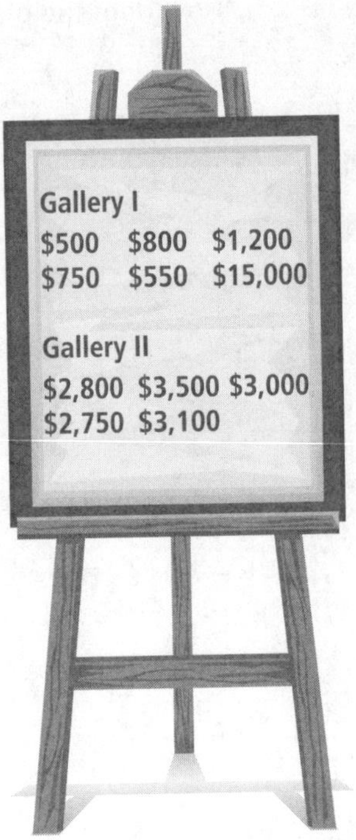

A. Do you agree with Stacy or Diego? Explain your reasoning.

B. Reasoning What reason(s) could there be for the differences in sales prices between the two galleries and for the outlier in Gallery I?

HABITS OF MIND

Make Sense and Persevere What is the mean sales price for the paintings at Gallery I? What is the mean sales price for the paintings at Gallery II?

Notes

Assess

EXAMPLE 1

Try It! Compare Data Sets Displayed in Dot Plots

1. How does the outlier in the second data set affect the mean and the MAD?

EXAMPLE 2

Try It! Compare Data Sets Displayed in Box Plots

2. How does the IQR compare to the range for each school?

HABITS OF MIND

Use Appropriate Tools Does the information given by a box plot allow you to determine the mean of a set of data?

EXAMPLE 3

Try It! Compare Data Sets Displayed in Histograms

3. If the marketing team wants to advertise a product that is targeted at adults 25–34, during which show should they advertise? Explain.

EXAMPLE 4

Try It! Make Observations With Data Displays

4. a. Provide a possible explanation for each of the observations that was made.

   b. Make 2 more observations about the data that Nadia collected.

HABITS OF MIND

Use Appropriate Tools Does the type of graph you create with given data change the observations that can be made from the data display? Explain.

Do You UNDERSTAND?

1. ESSENTIAL QUESTION How can you use measures of center and spread to compare data sets?

2. **Communicate Precisely** How are the MAD and the IQR similar? How are they different?

3. **Reason** When comparing two sets of data, it is common to look at the means. Why might the MAD be a useful piece of information to compare in addition to the mean?

4. **Error Analysis** Val says that if the minimum and maximum values of two data sets are the same, the median will be the same. Is Val correct? Explain.

Do You KNOW HOW?

Use the two data sets.

Data Set A

86	87	98	85	90
94	89	83	76	84
83	90	87	87	86

Data Set B

80	89	70	75	87
88	75	87	89	81
84	87	88	81	87

5. How do the means compare?

6. How do the MADs compare?

7. How do the medians compare?

8. How do the IQRs compare?

9. Which measures of center and spread are better for comparing data sets A and B? Explain.

Activity

10-3 Interpreting the Shapes of Data Displays

SavvasRealize.com

EXPLORE & REASON

A meteorologist looks at measures of center to summarize the last 10 days of actual high temperatures.

A. Find the median, mean, and mode of the data.

B. Which of the three measures of center seems to be the most accurate in describing the data? Explain.

C. Communicate Precisely How can you describe the data?

HABITS OF MIND

Reason Explain how the central tendencies of the data would shift if the temperatures 90°, 95°, and 95° were not included.

EXAMPLE 1

Try It! Interpret the Shape of a Distribution

1. Suppose a third category of dogs has a mean of 40 lb and a median of 32 lb. What can you infer about the shape of the histogram for the dogs in this category?

EXAMPLE 2

Try It! Interpret the Shape of a Skewed Data Display

2. How do skewed data affect the mean in this context?

HABITS OF MIND

Construct Arguments A student reasons that because most of the data in a histogram lie on the right side of the graph, the data must be skewed right. Is this student correct? Justify your answer.

Notes

Assess

EXAMPLE 3

Try It! Compare Shapes of Skewed Data Displays

3. What does the shape of the histogram for the second sample tell you about the data?

EXAMPLE 4

Try It! Interpret the Shape of a Symmetric Data Display

4. Suppose the quality control manager adds another 10 bagels to the third sample. If 5 of the bagels are 78 g each, and 5 of the bagels are 106 g each, would that affect the mean and median weights? Explain.

EXAMPLE 5

Try It! Comparing the Shapes of Data Sets

5. Suppose a fourth school district offers Jennifer a job. School District 401 has a mean salary of $57,000 and a median salary of $49,000. Should Jennifer consider accepting the job offer with School District 401? Explain.

HABITS OF MIND

Reason If the mean and median of a set of data are equal, or nearly equal, are the data necessarily symmetric? Explain.

Do You UNDERSTAND?

1. ESSENTIAL QUESTION How does the shape of a data set help you understand the data?

2. **Use Structure** How are the shapes of dot plots, histograms, and box plots similar? How are they different?

3. **Error Analysis** Nicholas says that the display for a skewed data distribution is symmetrical about the mean. Is Nicholas correct? Explain your reasoning.

Do You KNOW HOW?

Tell whether each display is skewed left, skewed right, or symmetric. Interpret what the display tells you about the data set.

4.

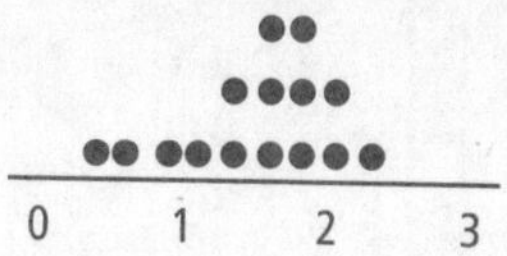

5.

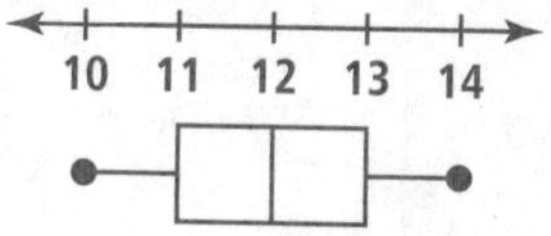

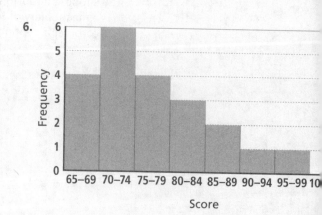

6.

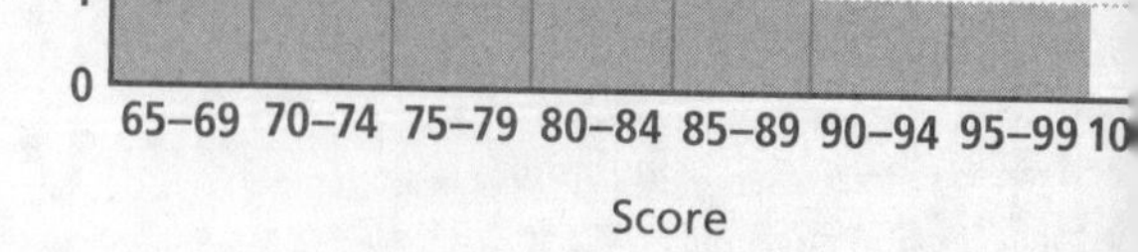

Activity

10-4 Standard Deviation

SavvasRealize.com

MODEL & DISCUSS

A meteorologist compares the high temperatures for two cities during the past 10 days.

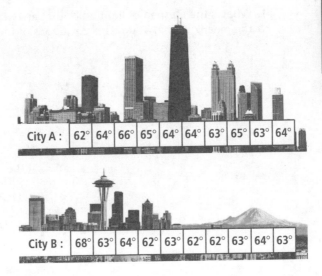

City A :	62°	64°	66°	65°	64°	64°	63°	65°	63°	64°

City B :	68°	63°	64°	62°	63°	62°	62°	63°	64°	63°

A. Create a data display for each city's high temperatures.

B. **Use Structure** What does the shape of each data display indicate about the data set and the measures of center?

HABITS OF MIND

Make Sense and Persevere What is the range of each data set? What is the mean of each data set?

Notes

Assess

EXAMPLE 1

Try It! Interpret the Variability of a Data Set

1. What is the lifespan of light bulbs that are within 2 standard deviations of the mean? Within 3 standard deviations of the mean?

HABITS OF MIND

Reason Does any of the data from Example 1 fall three standard deviations above or below the mean? In general, is it possible for data to fall more than two standard deviations above or below the mean? Explain.

Assess

EXAMPLE 2

Try It! Calculate the Standard Deviation of a Sample

2. The table shows the number of cars sold by the auto sales associate over the next eight-week period. How much variability do the data show?

12	14	29	10	17	16	18	16

EXAMPLE 3

Try It! Find Standard Deviation of a Population

3. What was the range of points that the team scored in 95% of their regular season games?

EXAMPLE 4

Try It! Compare Data Sets Using Standard Deviation

4. Compare Brand C, with mean 1,250 hours and standard deviation 83 hours, to Brands A and B.

HABITS OF MIND

Communicate Precisely What does a large standard deviation indicate?

Do You UNDERSTAND?

1. **ESSENTIAL QUESTION** Why does the way in which data are spread out matter?

2. **Generalize** What are the steps in finding standard deviation?

3. **Error Analysis** Marisol says that standard deviation is a measure of how much the values in a data set deviate from the median. Is Marisol correct? Explain.

4. **Use Structure** If you add 10 to every data value in a set, what happens to the mean, range, and standard deviation. Why?

Do You KNOW HOW?

Sample A: 1, 2, 2, 5, 5, 5, 6, 6

Sample B: 5, 9, 9, 10, 10, 10, 11, 11

5. What can you determine by using range to compare the spread of the two data sets?

6. Find the standard deviation for each data set.

7. How can you use standard deviation to compare the spread of each data set?

8. Based on the histogram, what data values are within one standard deviation of the mean?

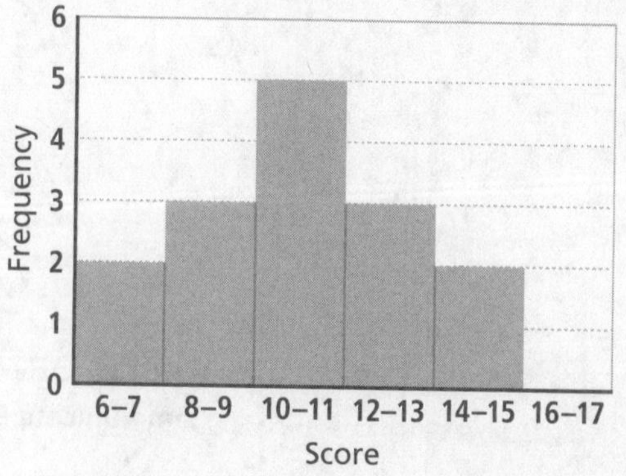

Mean: 11.05
Standard Deviation: 2.40

10-5 Two-Way Frequency Tables

SavvasRealize.com

Activity

EXPLORE & REASON

Baseball teams at a high school and a college play at the same stadium. Results for every game last season are given for both teams. There were no ties.

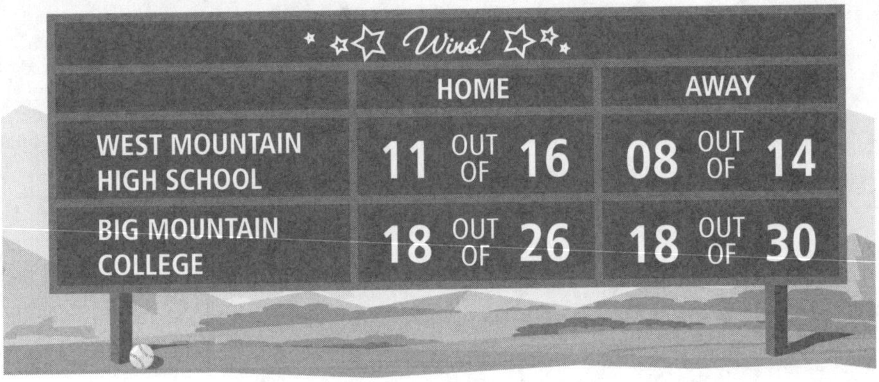

Wins!
HOME
AWAY
WEST MOUNTAIN HIGH SCHOOL
11 OUT OF 16
08 OUT OF 14
BIG MOUNTAIN COLLEGE
18 OUT OF 26
18 OUT OF 30

A. How could you organize the data in table form?

B. Look for Relationships How would you analyze the data to determine whether the data support the claim that the team that plays at home is more likely to win?

HABITS OF MIND

Make Sense and Persevere What percentage of the West Mountain High School team's total games are home wins? What percentage of the Big Mountain College team's total games are away losses?

Notes

Assess

EXAMPLE 1

Try It! Interpret a Two-Way Frequency Table

1. What do the marginal frequencies tell you about the number of male and female respondents?

EXAMPLE 2

Try It! Interpret a Two-Way Relative Frequency Table

2. How can you tell whether a greater percent of customers surveyed selected veggie burger or veggie pizza?

HABITS OF MIND

Communicate Precisely How does joint relative frequency relate to joint frequency? How does marginal relative frequency relate to marginal frequency?

EXAMPLE 3

Try It! Calculate Conditional Relative Frequency

3. What conclusion could the marketing team make about male and female preferences for veggie pizza? Justify your answer.

EXAMPLE 4

Try It! Interpret Conditional Relative Frequency

4. What conclusion could you draw if the percentages for male and female customers were the same across the rows in this table?

EXAMPLE 5

Try It! Interpret Data Frequencies

5. What does the conditional relative frequency $\frac{72}{137}$ represent in this context?

HABITS OF MIND

Look for Relationships Why can there be multiple values for the conditional relative frequency?

Assess

Do You UNDERSTAND?

1. ESSENTIAL QUESTION How can you use two-way frequency tables to analyze data?

2. **Communicate Precisely** How are joint frequencies and marginal frequencies similar? How are they different?

3. **Look for Relationships** How are conditional relative frequencies related to joint frequencies and marginal frequencies?

4. **Error Analysis** Zhang says that the marginal relative frequency for a given variable is 10. Could Zhang be correct? Explain your reasoning.

Do You KNOW HOW?

In a survey, customers select Item A or Item B. Item A is selected by 20 males and 10 females. Of 20 customers who select Item B, five are males.

5. Make a two-way frequency table to organize the data.

6. Make a two-way relative frequency table to organize the data.

7. Calculate conditional relative frequencies for males and females. Is it reasonable to conclude that males prefer Item A more than females do?

8. Calculate conditional relative frequencies for Item A and Item B. Is it reasonable to conclude that a customer who prefers Item B is more likely to be a female than a male?

Video

MATHEMATICAL MODELING IN 3 ACTS

SavvasRealize.com

Text Message

Text messages used be just that: text only. Now you can send multimedia messages (or MMS) with emojis, images, audio, and videos. Did you know Finland was the first country to offer text messaging to phone customers?

Some people send and receive so many texts that they use textspeak to make typing faster. RU 1 of them? You will see one person keep track of his text messages in this Modeling Mathematics in 3 Acts lesson.

ACT 1 Identify the Problem

1. What is the first question that comes to mind after watching the video?

2. Write down the Main Question you will answer about what you saw in the video.

3. Make an initial conjecture that answers this main question.

4. Explain how you arrived at your conjecture.

5. What information will be useful to know to answer the main question? How can you get it? How will you use that information?

Video

ACT 2 Develop a Model

6. Use the math that you have learned in this Topic to refine your conjecture.

ACT 3 Interpret the Results

7. Is your refined conjecture between the highs and lows you set up earlier?

8. Did your refined conjecture match the actual answer exactly? If not, what might explain the difference?